Apparitions of Jesus

The Resurrection as Ghost Story

Robert Conner

Tellectual Press
tellectual.com

Tellectual Press
tellectual.com
Valley, WA

Print ISBN: 978-1-942897-16-3

Tellectual Press is an imprint of Tellectual LLC.

Copyright © 2018 by Robert Conner

All rights reserved. Please do not make or keep unauthorized copies of this book.

Cover design by Edwin A. Suominen, based on an engraving by Gustav Doré ("The Ascension"). Done with The GIMP free image processing software.

Unless otherwise indicated, all quotations from the New Testament and other Greek sources were translated by the author.

Table of Contents

Introduction	**3**
Ghosts, Scholars, and Apologetics	5
Cultural Distance	8
Glossary	**13**
I: The Powers of the Dead	**17**
Conjuring Ghosts	21
Necromancy in the Old Testament	24
Christian necromancy	25
II: The Ghost Of John the Baptist	**31**
Ghosts as Magical Assistants	39
Jesus the Necromancer	41
III: An Abundance of Visions	**53**
A Bacchic Vision of Jesus?	54
The Stigmatic and His Visions	56
The Last Trumpet	57
Visions or Hallucinations?	59
1 Corinthians 15	69
IV: The Resurrection As Ghost Story	**85**
The Empty Tomb	85
Women as Witnesses	95
The Narrative Shifts	99
On the Road to Emmaus	104
"A ghost does not have flesh and bones"	109
"Though the doors were locked"	110
Jesus the Revenant?	114

I am the Translation and the Life	120
Back to Celsus	127
V: The Resurrection as Magic	**137**
A Christ with Calories	137
In the Name of Jesus Crucified	144
VI: Wrapping Up	**151**
A Personal Revelation	154
References	**157**
Index	**183**

Robert Conner studied Greek and Hebrew at Western Kentucky University from 1975 through 1977. Since 1983, he has published books and articles on electrocardiography, a novel, three books on magic in early Christianity, and a study of the "Secret" gospel of Mark controversy. He has always been fascinated with languages and enjoys reading the gospels in their original tongue.

He can be reached at **tragsbook@gmail.com**

Introduction

While reading Daniel Ogden's sourcebook[1] as background for my first book on magic in the career of Jesus, it occurred to me that some of the resurrection accounts of the gospels read a lot like Greco-Roman ghost stories. Although the parallels seemed clear, even unavoidable, my initial search of the periodical literature devoted to New Testament studies failed to turn up anything that specifically addressed the question. To my surprise, it seemed no one else had noticed these curious similarities, or at least had not ventured to publish on the subject.

Ghosts are something the writers of the New Testament definitely believed in. "Shortly before dawn Jesus went out to them, walking on the lake. When the disciples saw him walking on the lake, they were terrified. 'It's a ghost,' they said, and cried out in fear." (Matt. 14:25-26).[2] When Jesus appeared to his disciples after his resurrection we are informed, "They were startled and frightened, thinking they saw a ghost" (Luke 24:37, NIV).[3]

The parable of the Rich Man and Lazarus also presupposes that someone could rise from the dead to warn others: "He said to him, 'If they do not listen to Moses and the Prophets, they will not be convinced even if someone rises from the dead'" (Luke 16:31). A post-mortem afterlife is apparently presupposed by Jesus' reply, "Now about the dead rising—have you not read in the Book of Moses, in the account of the burning bush, how God said to him, 'I am the God of Abraham, the God of Isaac, and the God of Jacob'? He is not the God of the dead, but of the living" (Mark 12:26-27). The exorcism of "Legion" from the demoniac living "among the tombs" (Mark 5:2) may imply possession by ghosts since physical and mental illness were often attributed to ghosts of the "angry dead" and unhappy ghosts were also credited with inducing "suicidal insanity" among the vulnerable.[4]

My first foray into the subject of magic in the career of Jesus and the early church included a brief chapter, "The Resurrection As

Ghost Story,"[5] that pointed to the remarkable correspondence between the post-mortem appearances of Jesus in the narratives of Luke and John and ghost folklore from the ancient past. Several gospel passages have a conspicuous resemblance to ghost stories, so the relative lack of comment in the New Testament studies literature seemed hard to explain.

But further research on the topic revealed that I was far from the first to have noticed that the post-mortem sightings of Jesus were spectral in nature. Celsus, a Roman philosopher and opponent of Christianity who lived in the 2nd century, made *precisely* that observation 18 centuries ago–"[Celsus] considers the appearance of Jesus to his disciples after rising from the dead to be like *a ghost* (*phasma*) hovering before their sight."[6] More on that later.

Since 2006, at least two articles have appeared that specifically address the similarities of the gospel narratives to ghost lore. Deborah T. Prince, writing in the *Journal for the Study of the New Testament*, observes that Luke must have used "the vocabulary and literary models"[7] available to him–literary models that included ghost stories–and builds a strong case that Luke did exactly that. Daniel Smith, in an article in *The Catholic Biblical Quarterly* notes, "the materiality/physicality of Jesus' risen body in Luke . . . is not inconsistent with ancient descriptions of ghosts."[8]

On further investigation, I found that at least a few other writers appear to have *nearly* "gone there." Commenting on Luke's 'Road to Emmaus' story, historian Dale Allison points out that it "is reminiscent of modern urban legends about phantom hitchhikers who suddenly disappear, only after which their identities are learned,"[9] and says of collective visions, "Whether or not they are persuasive, the truth of the matter, welcome or not, is that the literature on visions of the dead is full of parallels to the stories we find in the Gospels."[10]

After a detailed and fully footnoted discussion of post-mortem apparitions as they may relate to the gospel stories, Allison concludes, "The unexpected appearance and disappearance of

Jesus, for instance, and the brevity of the speeches are par for the apparitional course. It is also credible that encounters with the risen Jesus, like some apparitions, produced doubt as well as belief, and likewise plausible that the earthly setting for the canonical stories is not a fiction, for apparitions are typically terrestrial."[11] While I do not wish to mischaracterize Allison's argument in any way, which I regard as well put, "ghost" and "apparition" are for all practical purposes interchangeable.

Writing in the *Tyndale Bulletin*, Ian Marshall first notes that "Luke is capable of considerable freedom in constructing scenes and stories"[12] and adds, "the appearance of a person who is dead to those still living is found in secular legends; the motifs of the divine being appearing in the form of a wanderer and/or appearing to wanderers and his sudden disappearance are also paralleled in legend."[13] It seems to me that this comes as close as possible to calling Luke's "Road to Emmaus" account a ghost story without actually calling it a ghost story. Robert Stein also observed, "the risen Christ does possess certain supernatural features. He can vanish (Luke 24:31), appear mysteriously (Luke 24:36), and go through closed doors (John 20:19)."[14]

Despite these exceptions, comparison of the resurrection narratives with nearly identical material from Greco-Roman ghost lore is not a common topic in the professional literature. There are several reasons why that might be the case.

Ghosts, Scholars, and Apologetics

Like other topics generally filed under the heading of the "paranormal," ghosts are a rather schlocky cast of characters, a perennial fascination of society's lower classes, and hardly the sort of subject most scholars from prestigious institutions deign to considerer–"Ghosts were, in a nutshell, embarrassing."[15] The reticence of scholars is at least partly understandable given the history of ghost studies–the ghost hunters of the 19th century, searching for proof of life after death, firmly established the link between apparitions conjured up by mediums in trances and fraud perpetrated upon grieving, vulnerable people.[16] Little wonder that most mainstream historians, working in a discipline dominated by rationalism and materialist explanation, have given short shrift to the superstitions of the hoi polloi and to supernaturalism in general.

More to the point, one could hardly expect Christian historians or biblical scholars with any degree of devotional allegiance to compare The Resurrection of the Lord to the appearance of ghosts. Merely to raise such a question not only offends Christian belief, it lacks deference to the religious sensibilities of others–possibly powerful others in positions to exact personal or professional retribution for speaking out of turn. As John Gager expressed it,

> A combination of theological, cultural, and historical factors have conspired to create a protected enclave for [Christianity]. As a consequence, methods and techniques that are taken for granted in the treatment of other religions have been ignored or discarded in dealing with this one ... the further assumption has been made, with however much sophistication, that certain events in early Christianity are not only historically distinctive but in some sense religiously unique ...[17]

Or as Richard Miller has pungently expressed the matter, study of the gospels is "a field overgrown with faith-based scholarship."[18]

For modern literalists, the bodily resurrection of Jesus is still "the central miracle in human history," and the "historically verifiable, bodily resurrection of Jesus the Lord must be defended in every generation–a perennial responsibility with great privilege as part of Gospel proclamation."[19] William Walker put the issue in stark terms: "If the first Christians were in error about [the resurrection], if God did not raise Jesus from the dead, then Christianity has no real basis and is a delusion."[20] Speaking on behalf of many, one writer declares, "the Easter resurrection is the absolutely inalienable presupposition of the gospel, for without it there would have been no gospel to be proclaimed."[21]

To assert that some of the resurrection accounts may have borrowed elements of common folklore implies that the gospel stories can be compared to similar stories from the ancient world. So this criticism of Robert Miller merits an extended quote:

> It is up to the evangelical camp to explain why hypothetical biographies extremely similar to the Gospels but not about Jesus should be met with sturdy skepticism, while every scholarly effort should be made to argue for the historical reliability of the canonical Gospels. Those of us in the traditional historical-Jesus camp are fairly certain that we already know why—and that the reason has little (or nothing) to do with historical method and a great deal (or everything) to do with theological presuppositions. Why else would the name of the hero make such a profound difference in the historical assessment of the stories in which the hero appears?[22]

Until quite recently, it bordered on sacrilege if not heresy or even atheism to suggest that a gospel writer—none of whom appears to have been an eyewitness of the events he purports to relate—may have filled in narrative gaps or invented stories outright using material taken from the surrounding culture. That said, it can be claimed with some assurance that "a rigid conceptual distinction" between the categories of fiction and history is a modern notion that "will have been quite alien to ancient readers."[23]

Disputes about the resurrection have raged within Christianity since its beginning, but within the past two hundred years an intellectual form of trench warfare has developed between those who favor the historical method of interrogation and those who champion theology as the deciding factor. Within the past few decades a tsunami of publications has debated whether something really happened to Jesus or whether something merely happened to his disciples.[24] That Luke and John may have incorporated ghost lore into their resurrection accounts brings us at least to the periphery of that debate.

In any case, the claim of resurrection posed serious historical, theological, and apologetic problems for early Christian believers–"mutual disagreement and dissension was already present among the first Christian communities for which we have evidence . . . The resurrection of Jesus, while affirmed by all Jewish Christians, could mean different things to different Jewish-Christian groups."[25] It would therefore come as little surprise that those who understood the resurrection to be the cornerstone of their faith turned to the cultural resources available to them in order to defend their belief.[26]

It's common knowledge that "the scriptures of Israel contribute language, motifs, and patterns for speaking of Jesus."[27] Besides the well known "proof texts" from the Hebrew Scriptures,[28] the resources in the folklore of the broader Greco-Roman culture were obviously available as well to literate gentile writers such as Luke. As Felton observes, folklore typically encompasses "units of traditional material that are memorable and consequently repeatable"[29] and ghost lore in particular is pervasive, nearly universal in character, and like the gospel material, "handed down to us" (Luke 1:2) from generation to generation–an example of "common social experience."

Like several other modern writers, I will argue in this book for "the interdependence of folklore and religion"[30] as the approach most likely to yield defensible conclusions. There is also evidence that for some Christian individuals and sects the claim of bodily resurrection was never of central importance and that doubt and difference of opinion persisted even among those for whom bodily resurrection was a core conviction,[31] a subject to which we will return.

Cultural Distance

The modern reader who seeks to understand the ancient view of ghosts encounters several formidable barriers. First, the surviving literary and archaeological sources generally are fragmentary, "a limited data base,"[32] a tiny percentage of what once existed. As for early Christian belief in particular, "the first 150 years of Christianity, say from 30 to 180 CE, are known only from textual or scribal remains."[33] More to the point, "Jesus left nothing in writing, and gave no charge to his followers to prepare a written record of his sayings or of his deeds. They were commissioned to preach, not to write . . ."[34]

As many as two generations passed, with a devastating regional war supervening, before the composition of the gospels. During that time, the oral tradition was embellished, Old Testament and "folk story themes" were incorporated into the tradition, which was then translated from Aramaic into Greek. Stories were conflated; their original contexts blurred or altogether lost, or were changed under "the influence of the church's situation."[35] As Rudhardt pointed out, the modern student of ancient cultures and their religions—despite familiarity with ancient religions and cultures—seems destined to remain a stranger in a strange land.[36]

Since New Testament narratives of Jesus' post-mortem appearances are the principal interest of this book, questions about the sources and reliability of those narratives are unavoidable. Regrettably for ancient history generally and for the history of Christianity specifically, however, the quest for origins is the pursuit of a misty phantom through a dense fog—"The further back we go in the history of the birth of the church the less the records have to tell us."[37]

Several factors have worked against the survival of written sources: the widespread destruction of the libraries of antiquity, the cost of copying books by hand before the invention of the printing press, and Christian contempt both for the pagan world that preceded it and the sects the winners regarded as heretical. We know many writers of the distant past only by name and many others have likely disappeared without a trace, their potential contribution to our understanding lost forever.

A further barrier to reconstructing ancient belief is the inconsistent nature of ancient belief itself. Like modern people, the ancients had a variety of logically inconsistent opinions on the subject of the afterlife and those opinions evolved over time.[38] As noted by Felton in her study of ancient ghost lore, "there simply was no consensus concerning what ghosts consisted of or how they could make themselves seen."[39] Nevertheless, the majority clearly took ghosts and their powers seriously, much more so than modern Westerners. It is difficult if not impossible for most modern readers to fully appreciate the role the dead played in the popular culture of the ancient world. Part of the objective of this book must be to sketch the context of that social world.

Finally, there is the significant language barrier. Most of the primary sources at our disposal, at least the ones I will be referencing, are in Greek. So far as we can tell, all the documents of the New Testament were originally composed by speakers of Greek. We must sort through some of the ideas that Greek speakers held about ghosts, not to mention the modern *interpretations* of those ideas. And we are confronted with quite a variety of terms for the dead.

Even as English speakers use *ghost*, *specter*, *shade*, *spook*, *soul*, *apparition*, *phantom*, *wraith*, and so on to refer to the dead (without much distinction in meaning), Greek also employed a number of terms of overlapping meaning to refer to ghosts.[40] Insofar as possible I reproduce Greek terms with the English alphabet, including referenced resource material. To help readers navigate the welter of terms for the dead, I've included a brief glossary of relevant vocabulary that follows this introduction, a glossary I hope will help to orient readers who wish to expand their inquiry.

Notes

1. Ogden, *Magic, Witchcraft, and Ghosts in the Greek and Roman Worlds*, 2002, Oxford University Press.

INTRODUCTION

2. See Combs on the narrative function of the "ghost on the water" in Mark *Journal of Biblical Literature* 127 (2008) 345-58.

3. Louw and Nida list *phantasma, ghost,* or *apparition* as a synonym of *pneuma, spirit,* and note, "the psychological phenomena associated with such appearances are apparently universal." *Greek Lexicon of the New Testament Based on Semantic Domains,* I, 147.

4. Johnston, *Restless Dead,* 107, 228.

5. Conner, *Jesus the Sorcerer: Exorcist and Prophet of the Apocalypse,* 2006, Mandrake of Oxford, 63-72.

6. Origen, *Contra Celsum* VII, 35.

7. Prince, *Journal for the Study of the New Testament* 29 (2007) 297.

8. Smith, *The Catholic Biblical Quarterly* 72 (2010) 754.

9. Allison, *Resurrecting Jesus,* 253.

10. Ibid, 270.

11. Ibid, 286.

12. Marshall, *Tyndale Bulletin* 24 (1973) 79.

13. Ibid, 80.

14. Stein, *Journal of Biblical Literature* 95 (1976) 92.

15. Clarke, *Ghosts: A Natural History,* 174.

16. Ibid, particularly the chapter "The Thrilling of the Tables," 181-206.

    The efforts of early psychic investigators to expose fraud is described in detail by Deborah Blum. *Ghost Hunters,* 57-58, 91, 138-40, 244-48.

17. Gager, *Kingdom and Community,* xi, 3.

18. Miller, *Journal of Biblical Literature* 129 (2010) 759.

19. Cabal, *The Southern Baptist Journal of Theology* 18 (2014) 116.

20. Walker, *Journal of Biblical Literature* 88 (1969) 157.

21. Beasley-Murray, *Tyndale Bulletin* 42 (1991) 296.

22. Miller, *Journal for the Study of the Historical Jesus* 9 (2011) 92-93.

23. Francis, *American Journal of Philology* 119 (1998) 421.

24. Craffert, *Journal for the Study of the Historical Jesus* 7 (2009) 126-29.

25. Riley, *Resurrection Reconsidered,* 2, 22.

26. I have found only one comprehensive reference that attempts to organize the vast amount of published material on the subject of the passion and resurrection, *The Resurrection: A Critical Inquiry* (Alter, 2015), a massive trove that contains a healthy bibliography of some 81 pages.

27. Aitken, *Harvard Theological Review* 90 (1997) 370.

28. Psalm 22 and Isaiah 53 proved particularly susceptible to such an apologetic interpretation.
29. Felton, *Haunted Greece and Rome*, 1.
30. Ibid, 4, 41.
31. A discussion of the evolving theology of the resurrection of the body is not our immediate concern. For a survey of the conflicting explanations see Grant, *The Journal of Religion* 28 (1948) 120-30, 188-208.
32. Schmidt, *Israel's Beneficent Dead*, 4.
33. Crossan, *Numen* 39 (1992) 233.
34. Beare, *Journal of Biblical Literature* 87 (1968) 125.
35. Ibid, 128-29.
36. Rudhardt, *Numen* 11 (1964) 189-211.
37. Snape, *Numen* 17 (1970) 188.
38. Rice & Stambaugh, *Sources for the Study of Greek Religion*, 163.

    See also Finucane, *Ghosts*, 9-10.
39. Felton, op. cit., 21. See particularly her chapter "Problems of Definition and Classification," 22-37.
40. There were even Greek terms for ghosts that attacked "women and babies," such as "*gellō, lamia, mormō, mormolukē*, and *strix*." Johnston, *Restless Dead*, 164.

Glossary

agamos (Greek): *unmarried.* "Already in Homer, there are allusions to the belief that the unmarried dead were excluded from the Underworld and might harm the living."[1]

agunaios (Greek): *wifeless, unmarried.*

alastōr (Greek): an *avenging spirit.*

aōros (Greek): *Untimely, premature*, in reference to death before one's *appointed hour* (*ōra*). The prematurely deceased, including miscarriages and those who died in infancy, were widely regarded as likely to become restless ghosts. "The group most commonly called *aōroi* are women who die without marrying and bearing and nurturing children."[2]

apaidēs (Greek): *childless. Gello*, for example, is "the soul of a dead virgin who wandered around in the world of the living, enviously killing babies and pregnant women."[3]

ataphos (Greek): *unburied.* Specifically, *those who fail to receive due funeral rites.* The *ataphoi* (pl) included soldiers missing in action, sailors lost at sea whose bodies are never recovered, and those dishonored by deliberate refusal of burial. The Greeks were honoring and appeasing the unburied dead with *cenotaphs*–from *kenos* (*empty*) and *taphos* (*tomb*)–long before moderns raised such monuments to their fallen "long gray lines of brothers."

biaiothanatos (Greek): *violently killed, executed.* The *biaiothanatoi* (pl) as a class were regarded as potential instruments of black magic. This category also included victims of accidental death such death due to lightning that were "regarded . . . as the victims of hostility of invisible forces."[4]

daimōn, (Greek): broadly, a *supernatural being* which could include a "tutelary spirit" or "phantom." The term could also be used of "destiny, fate," or "genius, inner voice."[5]

di parentes (Latin): *spirits of the ancestors*.

eidōlon (Greek): *apparition, phantasm, specter, appearance, simulacrum, reflected image*, used interchangeably with *psychē,* "soul." The soul preserves the *image* (*eidōlon*) of what the person was in life.

energeō (Greek): *act, accomplish, perform, operate*. This is the verb that dissolves all distinctions between miracle and magic, used both in the New Testament as well as the magical papyri for "activating" magical spells as well as miracles.

Erinys (Greek): "the Erinys was primarily the angry ghost, and a ghost is never so angry as when he has been murdered."[6] In time the Erinys, "all but identified with the dead man's curse which finally brought his injurer to justice,"[7] morph into the *Furies*, crones charged with avenging wrongs, particularly crimes against relatives.

eudeipnia (Greek), literally *good supper*, an offering to the souls of the dead.

larva(*e*) (Latin): *malevolent ghost, spectre*; *larvatus* (adj.) *bewitched, enchanted*.

lemur(*es*) (Latin): *resentful* and *malevolent ghosts* propitiated during *Lemuria*, a festival celebrated on May 9th, 11th, and 13th. The Romans considered marriage during May unlucky because joy and celebration attracted the attention of the resentful dead.

miastōr (Greek): *avenger* of crime.

nekudaemōn (Greek): a *spirit of the dead*. The word occurs frequently in the spells of the magical papyri.

ōb (Hebrew): *ghost, ancestral spirit*.

paredros (Greek): *helper*, [magical] *assistant*. The *paredroi* (pl) included all sorts of spirit entities including angels, gods, ghosts, and heroes.

phantasma (Greek): *ghost, apparition, phantom, dream, vision*. The term occurs twice in the New Testament at Mark 6:49 and Matthew 14:26.

phasma (Greek): an *apparition, phantom, specter*, but also used for "sign, prodigy, omen."[8]

prostropaios (Greek): an *avenging spirit*, the ghost of a victim of crime, a ghost that returns to punish or take revenge, "the spirit of a murdered person that seeks vengeance for his death... the spirits of murdered persons, which pursue homicides with vengeance."[9]

psyche (Greek): *soul*, used with the same lack of precision as modern people.[10]

Notes

1. Johnston, op.cit., 22.
2. Ibid, 152.
3. Ibid, 22.
4. Lecouteux, *The Return of the Dead*, 15.
5. Montanari, *The Brill Dictionary of Ancient Greek*, 450.
6. Harrison, *Journal of Hellenic Studies* 19 (1899) 208.
7. Fairbanks, *American Journal of Philology* 21 (1900) 244.
8. Montonari, op. cit., 2258.
9. Hatch, *Harvard Studies in Classical Philology* 19 (1908) 183, 186.
10. The term could encompass emotions, or even be considered part of the body. See LiDonnici, *Greek, Roman, and Byzantine Studies* 39 (1998) 70-74.

I

The Powers of the Dead

The ancient peoples of the Mediterranean basin–Egyptians, Hebrews, Greeks and Romans–feared the powers of the dead. It was a fear expressed in part by annual rituals of propitiation. Even during the flowering of Greek civilization, "the Grecian spring," the dead cast their shadow across the affairs of the living. As historian Ronald Finucane observes, "amidst all this intellectual and aesthetic brilliance, ghosts learned to walk by night, to haunt houses, to frighten grown men, to demand–and get–sacrifices ... Men still call up ghosts, but now ghosts also call upon men."[1]

The Greek *Anthesteria* festival–the name refers to the blooming of grape vines–was celebrated in Athens and other cities at the beginning of spring. Oddly enough, during this festival of Dionysus that functioned much like our Halloween, everyone took precautions against ghosts "imagined to wander freely in the upper world ... released from the bonds that normally held them close to their graves."[2] During the festival, "ghosts of the dead emerged from the underworld and entered the city,"[3] a supernatural event not unlike that reported in connection with Jesus' resurrection in which the dead emerged from their tombs "and went into the holy city" (Matt. 27:52).

In Rome, the *Parentalia*, a commemoration of the *di parentes* or spirits of the family dead, began on February 13 and ended nine days later with the *Feralia*, the ritual placation and exorcism of the *lemures*, "the night-wandering shades of the prematurely dead" or "shades of those who had a violent death."[4] Vengeance for homicide is a frequent cause for the appearance of ghosts since the dead are not truly dead until they are avenged–"murderers are particularly liable to be haunted by their victims."[5] The *dies Parentales*, the days of remembrance of dead family members, were also days of ill omen–*dies nefastus*–assemblies did not meet and legal proceedings were suspended.[6]

At the end of *Lemuria*, May 13, family ghosts thought to have returned to their homes were expelled when the *pater familias*, the head of the household, making the gesture of the *cornuto*, a clenched fist with index finger and little finger extended, concluded a ritual of exorcism with the ninefold repetition of the invocation "*Manes excite paterni*!"–"Ancestral spirits be gone!" Because potentially hostile spirits lurked about, the Romans also considered the entire month of May an unlucky time to contract a marriage.

As in the Latin West, an ambivalent attitude towards the dead was common in the Greek-speaking East where sorrow for the deceased combined with apprehension. The attitudes of the living regarding the dead have never been entirely logical; even though the dead were commonly believed to have moved on to a remote afterlife, they are also believed to retain a connection to the grave. "The whole fabric of belief about the 'unquiet grave' rests upon this assumption of corpse-spirit unity after death... pilgrims frequented the graves of good men and heroes for precisely the same reason–because the spirit was active in the vicinity of his bones."[7] The *bothros*, a pit for sacrificial offerings to raise ghosts and deities of the underworld, might take the form of a small bench with a hollow in the center placed before a tomb,[8] a place where food offerings might be left in much the same way that modern people place flowers on a grave.

Certain classes of the dead were not only likely to become restless ghosts, those ghosts could be summoned into the realm of the living to accomplish dark ends. "Like many peoples, the Greeks believed from a very early time that some special dead, such as the unburied and those who had died young, were angry with the living and had some means of harming them... the dead can be called back into action by the living in a variety of ways, including some that we might label 'magical.'"[9] Various diseases were attributed to "ghostly possession" and spirits of the dead "are often implicated in magico-religious texts as the cause of illness."[10]

Because "to die prematurely is a curse," all sorts of misfortune, including "epidemics and cases of madness and possession"[11] were attributed to the dead. The suffering of the living, physical illness or emotional distress, might be imputed to the angry dead–"victims of murder, or someone deprived of proper burial is harassing the living."[12]

Those who died before achieving life's goals, particularly marriage and childbearing, or who died prematurely or violently, were especially likely to become harmful ghosts–"Needy and dangerous figures waiting in the shadows of existence... particularly those who died young or violently, the unhappy and unsatisfied dead with their restless energy and free-floating rage."[13] The categories of the *unquiet ghost* or *nekudaimōn* included the *aōros* or *untimely* dead, the *biaiothanatos*, the *dead by violence* whose numbers included both the murdered and the executed–"part of a wider class of the restless dead who came to be thought of as the typical instruments of malign magic"[14]–as well as the *ataphos, unburied*, the *agamos, unmarried, agunaios*, or *wifeless*, and the *apaidēs*, or *childless*. The wifeless and childless may have been included because there would have been no survivors to tend to and visit the tomb of the deceased. The ghosts of the dead were sometimes conjured at their tombs with a formula that typically began, "I adjure you, ghost..."[15]

The use of body parts for black magic is widely attested and, as Aubert observes, "the bodily parts and fluids of most adults were probably considered of inferior quality compared to those of chaste individuals who had met an untimely death [aōroi]. In this context youngsters, both newborn and still-born babies, and embryos played an important rôle in magic."[16] Christianity carried this practice forward in spirit as evidenced by the miraculous cures and other wonders attributed to the preserved body parts–"relics"–of desexualized saints.

Across time and culture one repeatedly encounters "three types of dead" who are "always presumed to be dangerously restless:"[17] those who have not received proper rites, who lie unburied on the battlefield or are lost at sea, those who die before the normal span of life, and those who die violently. Euripides' *Hecuba* opens with the appearance of the ghost of Polydorus: "pounded by the surf, my corpse still lies, carried up and down on the heaving swell of the sea, unburied and unmourned . . . I shall appear, so that at last my body can be buried."[18] It is probably not coincidental that religious martyrs typically fall within one or more of these categories of restless ghosts.

Those who died before their allotted time, or had not completed the usual rites of passage–adulthood, marriage, childbearing, and old age–or had failed to receive the rituals necessary to send them into the afterlife, could return to haunt the living. They were objects of fear.

The notion that some classes of the dead roam freely at certain times of the year survived in medieval Europe under various names such as the *Wilde Jagd* or *Wildes Heer*, the "Wild Hunt" or "Wild Horde" which the Church taught was composed of the ghosts of "sinners, criminals, unbaptized children, people who had died without the sacraments or who died unrepentant."[19] The murdered dead were particularly dangerous. Among the "prodigies that terrified Rome" when Julius Caesar crossed the Rubicon were "the ghosts of the Samnites" who have "come to destroy the hated city, to fulfill, dead, what they had failed to accomplish living . . . Rome will be sacked by the ghosts of her victims."[20]

The ancients erected both spatial and ritual barriers between the living and the dead who, until the Christian era, were rarely buried in proximity to the living. The dead had their own "city," the necropolis, typically apart from the city of the living and distinguished from it. Among the Greeks, legislation limited the public display and ostentation of funerals as well as limiting the number of participants. It was probably to emphasize that the "dead and gone" were, in fact, *gone*, the body in the ground, the soul well and truly departed, and that "the individual no longer belonged amongst the living."[21] In the Christian social economy, burial in "consecrated ground was understood to be an apotropaic means,"[22] a measure to ward off spectral visitations.

Conjuring Ghosts

Those remaining above ground were not just troubled by the prospect of being harassed by spectral visits from the angry dead. The departed could be summoned back by necromancy to exert their power over the living.

The manipulation of spirits of the dead, "powerful to work good or evil to surviving men,"[23] was standard magical practice for centuries before the time of Jesus. Every culture of the Middle East and Mediterranean appears to have shared the belief that the ghosts of those who had died before achieving life's goals, particularly if they died violently, were earth-bound sources of enormous power. Conjuring dead heroes would seem to have developed logically from gravesites of notable figures functioning as early cult centers.[24] The best evidence suggests that death for the ancients represented "the separation of the spiritual and corporeal elements of man" and that the spirit "continued to live in close connection with the corpse and even depending on it."[25]

A spell from the magical papyri prescribes an invocation to raise a ghost as a magician's *paredros* or helper:

> I command you, *ghost of the dead* (*nekudaimon*), by the powerful and implacable god and by his holy names, to stand beside me in the night to come, in whatever form you had, and if you are able, transact for me [named] deed if I command you, now, now, quick, quick ... and he will actually stand alongside you in your dreams, throughout the night, and he will ask you, saying, "Command what you wish and I will do it."[26]

Defixiones or *katadesmoi*, inscribed lead sheets, often "folded up or rolled, pierced with an iron nail"[27] were deposited in great numbers in or near graves, and "the graves of *aōroi*, those who had died prematurely, were particularly popular" based on the determination of age from skeletal remains and gifts left in the grave.[28] The raising and invocation of ghosts and the gods of the underworld were literally works of darkness–"the graver and blacker was the business, the more near midnight was the hour,"[29] –and certain caves as well as lakes served as oracles where ghosts could be evoked.[30]

That necromancy was known among the Jews of Jesus' era is certain, as spells from the *Sepher Ha-Razim* make clear:

> These are the angels that obey (you) during the night (if you wish) to speak with the moon or the stars or to question a ghost or to speak with the spirits... If you wish to question a ghost; stand facing a tomb and repeat the names of the angels of the fifth encampment... I adjure you, O spirit of the ram bearer,[31] who dwells among the graves upon the bones of the dead."[32]

According to Deuteronomy, there were not only augurs and soothsayers, diviners and sorcerers, but also spell casters, necromancers, mediums, and people who sacrificed their own children in "the land of promise" (Deut. 18:9-14). As for the pious contention that a religiously pure Palestinian Judaism had been contaminated by the magical practice of neighboring peoples, Naveh and Shaked note,

> Palestine and Mesopotamia had two separate [magical] traditions, each with its own style and set of formulae. When however formulae from the two geographical areas converge, it may be invariably established the origin of the theme is Palestinian rather than Babylonian... Jewish incantation texts very often make use of biblical verses. This phenomenon is clearly visible in all varieties of Jewish magic, in the Mesopotamian bowls, the Palestinian amulets, as well as the magic material from

the Cairo genizah, and is also widely attested in late medieval and modern Jewish magical practice.[33]

Magical amulets are mentioned in Isaiah. The textual evidence suggests the presence of "a regular profession of enchanter"[34]–"the skillful magician and the expert in charms ... the headdresses, the armlets, the sashes, the perfume boxes, and the amulets" (Isa. 3:3, 20).[35]

As a rule, magic appears to have been the last resort of the lower strata of society; in the past as today, the members of the higher social orders worked their will through wealth and influence. But the case of Saul and the ghost raiser of Endor illustrates that even the powerful turned to magic if nothing else worked (1 Sam. 28:3-25). Material from excavated tombs provides support for a detail of the story of the evocation of Samuel's ghost–"An old man wearing a robe is coming up" (1 Sam. 28:14). Some individuals in Judean burials were buried wearing robes "as evidenced by ... the presence of toggle pins and fibulae in burials."[36]

Since the members of the lower classes were not only poor but generally illiterate, the magical workings of the commoners were unlikely to leave a written record or permanent residue for archaeologists to recover. If magical ritual consisted primarily of verbal activity with some manipulation of common materials, it would leave no distinctive trace of its existence.[37]

But there are, as noted by Schürer, various lines of evidence indicating that "magic flourished among the Jews despite strong and persistent condemnation by the religious authority. Healing by this means was especially common." He cites the story of Tobias expelling "the demon who threatened to ruin his wedding night" as reflecting "actual, contemporary, magical practice," especially given that it was done on "the advice of the angel Raphael" (Tobit 6:3-9, 17-1; 8:1-3). And, Schürer notes, Josephus in *Antiquities* VIII 2,5 "gives a sharply observed account of an exorcism, which he himself witnessed, performed by a Jew called Eleazar in the presence of Vespasian and his officers."[38]

Necromancy in the Old Testament

"When someone tells you to consult mediums and spiritists, who whisper and mutter, should not a people inquire of their God? Why consult the dead on behalf of the living?" (Isa. 8:19). According to Schmidt, this passage "potentially provides us with the earliest biblical tradition concerning the Israelite practice of necromancy."[39] A law against mediums and conjuring ghosts clearly presupposes not only the belief but also the practice. How otherwise to explain the command, "A man or woman who is a medium or spiritist among you must be put to death. You are to stone them; their blood will be on their own heads" (Lev. 20:27).

However, "in only two instances is a practitioner explicitly mentioned... In Deut[eronomy] 18:11, the necromancer is described as "one who asks of 'the One-who-returns and the Knower' or 'one who consults the dead.' In 1 Sam[uel] 28:7, the woman of Endor is named 'the controller of the One-who-returns.'" Schmidt notes a second example of necromancy in Isaiah 8:19-22, "the calling up of the deceased for purposes of ascertaining the unknown or predicting the future... in necromancy the active presence of the ghost is desired."[40] That certain dead were considered "divine beings" or literally "gods" is certain: "'Elōhîm ["gods"] is unequivocally used for the dead Samuel in the story of the woman of En-Dor (1 Samuel 28). Isaiah 8:19 provides a second example of 'elōhîm referring to the dead."[41]

There are a number of other references to necromancy in the Old Testament in addition to Saul's famous consultation with the ghost of Samuel.[42] A passage in Isaiah–"Brought low, you will speak from the ground; your speech will mumble out of the dust. Your voice will come ghost-like from the earth; out of the dust your speech will whisper" (Isa. 29:4)–together with the aforementioned evocation of Samuel's ghost, "establish the belief in the efficacy of the art of necromancy in at least some sectors of Israelite society."[43]

One of Israel's kings, Manasseh, "sacrificed his own son in the fire, practiced divination, sought omens, and consulted mediums and spiritists" (2 Kings 21:6). His successor, Josiah, "slaughtered all the priests of those high places on the altars and burned human bones on them ... Furthermore, Josiah got rid of the mediums and spiritists, the household gods, the idols and all the other detestable things seen in Judah and Jerusalem" (2 Kings 23:20, 24). Evidently the practice of necromancy had become so thoroughly engrained in Israelite society that violent measures were required to suppress it.

The Israelite ghost whisperer is a *shoel ōb*, or "one who consults an *ōb*." A term that often occurs with *ōb* is *yiddoni*, derived from the verb meaning *to know*. Davies conjectured that the word pair means "a ghost that knows."[44] The academic consensus is that the reference is to a ghost that is "knowledgeable and therefore able to answer the questions of the inquirer,"[45] "ghosts who have superior knowledge of the affairs of the living,"[46] "ancestral spirits"[47] conjured up for interrogation about the future. Interestingly enough, "the divine office of Jesus was recognized from the first by the demons, who, being of the spiritual world, were gifted with true discernment."[48]

Christian necromancy

Christian veneration of the Church of the Holy Sepulcher aside, there is no indication early Christians knew the location of Jesus' tomb. That's an odd omission if women both saw where Jesus was buried and visited the site! In the centuries that followed, however, Christians reverted to the ancient practice of incubation, "congregating in tombs that had acquired reputations as sites of martyrs' relics" and sleeping in tombs to "question the dead about the living."[49]

The earliest record of Christians collecting relics is found in *The Martyrdom of Saint Polycarp* of the 2nd century. There, the author describes how Polycarp's bones were gathered up after his body burned: "So afterward we collected his bones, more valuable than the most precious stones, more excellent than gold, and put them aside for ourselves in a suitable place."[50]

The 4th century writer Eunapius captures the revulsion of many pagans who witnessed the Christian practice of adoring relics and graves.

> They gathered up the bones and skulls of those apprehended for numerous crimes, men the courts had condemned, and proclaimed them to be gods, wallowed around their tombs, and declared that being defiled by graves made them stronger. The dead were called "martyrs," and some kind of "ministers," and "ambassadors of the gods," these degraded slaves, eaten alive by whips, their ghosts bearing the wounds of torture.[51]

"The *Proconsular Acts of Cyprian* tell us that the martyr-bishop's congregation spread cloths and napkins to catch the blood that fell as the saint was beheaded"[52]–the martyr's blood keeps him magically present. The Christian practice is brother to the evocation of ghosts described in the Greek magical papyri: "Facing the setting sun while holding material from the tomb, say, '... I summon the ruler of heaven and earth, Chaos and Hades, and the ghosts of men ... send this ghost to [me] from whose corpse I hold the remains in my hands.'"[53]

The adoration of relics still retained in cathedrals continues the practice in spirit, so to speak. "In the eyes of a pagan, Christianity was a religion of tombs."[54] The modern skeptic could easily conclude, as does Ritner, "Contemporary veneration of saintly relics–with invocations, visions and healings–is 'necromancy' by definition, but not by name."[55]

Notes

1. Finucane, *Ghosts: Appearances of the Dead*, 5.

2. Johnston, op. cit., 64.

See Ferguson, *Backgrounds in Early Christianity*, 243-51, for a useful summary of funerary beliefs and practices.

3. Felton, op. cit., 12.

"There is unambiguous testimony that the day of the Choes [the second day of Anthesteria, my note] was a 'day of pollution' ... People would start the day by chewing–contrary to all natural predilection–on leaves of a particular hawthorn variety ... which were otherwise used to ward off ghosts ... A little Choes pitcher was placed in the grave of any child who died before it was three, so that it could at least reach the goal symbolically in the next life which it had failed to reach in this one. This was analogous to the placement of the Loutrophoros, the water jug for the bridal bath, on the tomb of one who had died before marriage." Burkert, *Homo Necans*, 218, 221.

4. Thaniel, *The American Journal of Philology* 94 (1973) 182.

5. Kittredge, *American Journal Philology* 6 (1885) 163.

6. Dolansky, *Phoenix* 65 (2011) 128.

7. Finucane, op. cit., 8.

8. Rose, *Harvard Theological Review* 43 (1950) 261.

9. Johnston, op. cit., 30-31. For the Mesopotamian origins of many ghost beliefs see particularly "Magical Solutions to Deadly Problems," Johnston, *Restless Dead*, 83-90.

10. Adams, *Current Research in Egyptology 2006*, 12.

11. Lecouteux, op. cit., 12-13.

12. Burkert, *Ancient Mystery Cults*, 24.

13. Rabinowitz, *The Rotting Goddess*, 104.

14. Gordon, *Witchcraft and Magic in Europe: Ancient Greece and Rome*, 176.

15. Jordan, *Greek, Roman, and Byzantine Studies* 40 (1999) 165-66.

16. Aubert, *Greek, Roman, and Byzantine Studies* 30 (1989) 435.

17. Johnston, op. cit., 127.

18. *Hecuba* 27-29, 47.

19. Lecouteux, op. cit., 94.

20. Bagnani, *Phoenix* 9 (1955) 31.

21. Johnston, op. cit., 40.

22. Lecouteux, op. cit., 39, 101.

23. Fairbanks, op. cit., 248.

24. Wright, *Vetus Testamentum* 22 (1972) 476-86.

25. Renehan, *Greek, Roman, and Byzantine Studies* 21 (1980) 105.

26. Preisendanz, *Papyri Graecae Magicae* IV, 2030-2053.

    Ghosts are frequently invoked in erotic spells. Pachoumi, "The Erotic and Separation Spells of the Magical Papyri and *Defixiones*," *Greek, Roman, and Byzantine Studies* 53 (2013) 294-325.

27. Faraone, *Journal of Hellenic Studies* 105 (1985) 151.

28. Johnston, op. cit, 71.

29. Headlam, *Classic Review* 16 (1902) 52.

30. Ogden, *Acta Classica* 44 (2001), 167-195.

    The *Ploutōnia* "are places of access to the lower world, where souls of the dead are evoked." Fairbanks, "The Chthonic Gods of Greek Religion," *American Journal of Philology* 21 (1900) 247.

31. A reference to Hermes, a *psychopomp*, or guide of the dead.

32. Morgan, *Sepher Ha-Razim*, 36, 38.

33. Naveh & Shaked, *Magic Spells and Formulae*, 19-22.

34. Spoer, *Journal of Biblical Literature* 23 (1904) 97.

35. Compare Jeremiah 8:17, Ecclesiastes 10:11.

36. Bloch-Smith, *Journal of Biblical Literature* 111 (1992) 218.

37. Bohak, *Ancient Jewish Magic: A History*, 116-18, 137-38.

38. Schürer, *The History of the Jewish People in the Age of Jesus Christ*, III, I, 342.

39. Schmidt, *Israel's Beneficent Dead*, 147.

40. Schmidt, op. cit., 153-54.

41. Bloch-Smith, op. cit., 220.

42. For a discussion of the various solutions to the problems of the story, see Smelik, *Vigiliae Christianae* 33 (1977) 160-79.

43. Schmidt, op. cit., 202.

44. Davies, *Magic, Divination, and Demonology*, 89.

45. Jeffers, *Magic and Divination*, 172.

46. Schmidt, op. cit., 154.

47. Tropper, *Dictionary of Deities and Demons in the Bible*, 1524-30.

48. Scott, *Journal of Bible and Religion* 12 (1944) 20.

49. Frankfurter, *Harvard Theological Review* 103 (2010) 31-32

50. *Martyrdom of Saint Polycarp, Bishop of Smyrna*, XVIII, 2.

51. Eunapius, *Lives of the Philosophers and Sophists* (my translation).
52. Grig, *Making Martyrs in Late Antiquity*, 87.
53. Preisendanz, op. cit., 435, 443-49.
54. Burkert, *Ancient Mystery Cults*, 28.
55. Ritner, *Magic and Divination in the Ancient World*, 96.

II
The Ghost Of John the Baptist

> And Herod heard of it, for [Jesus'] name became known and they were saying, "John the Baptist has been raised from the dead and because of this the powers are at work in him."
>
> But others said, "He is Elijah," but others said, "A prophet, like one of the former prophets." But when Herod heard, he said, "John, the one I beheaded, this one has been raised."
>
> —Mark 6:14-16

The earliest gospel tells us that as Jesus' fame for exorcism and healing spread, Herod Antipas, the ruler of Galilee, became aware of it and, like others, sought an explanation for "such powerful works" (Mark 6:2). By the time his reputation came to Herod's attention, Jesus had passed his power over spirits to select disciples and began sending them out in pairs to preach and drive out demons—"he gave them authority over unclean spirits" (Mark 6:7, 13).

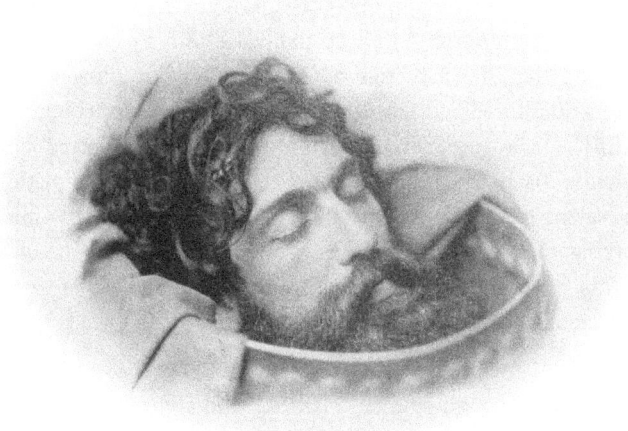

Study of the the Head of John the Baptist in a Charger[1]

As a result, the source of Jesus' authority became a topic of great interest. Some proposed that Jesus was Elijah returned from the dead, or "a prophet like one of the former prophets," but Herod had a different explanation: "John, the one I beheaded, has been raised."

A naïve reading of the text might lead us to assume that Herod thought Jesus was simply John the Baptist returned from the dead. But that is most unlikely. The careers of Jesus and John overlapped, and Herod had previously protected John (Mark 6:20). The early tradition is clear that Jesus began to preach and perform works of power after John had been imprisoned but before his eventual execution. Asked by John's disciples if he is the "one who is to come," Jesus replies,

> "When you go back, report what you hear and see to John. The blind are receiving sight and the lame walk about, lepers are being cleansed and the deaf hear and the dead are being raised and the poor receive the good news." (Matt. 11:3-5)

Herod–"that fox" (Luke 13:32)–was a Roman client whose position depended on his ability to keep the peace in his province, so it is probable that the activities of John, a popular preacher, were closely monitored and that "the crowds going out to be baptized by [John]" (Luke 3:7) contained informants who reported John's activities back to Herod. Representatives of the authorities in Jerusalem came down to Galilee in response to Jesus' miracle working (Mark 3:22), likely as a result of his ability to attract crowds–according to Mark the "whole town" gathered at the door of Simon's mother-in-law when word of a miracle spread (Mark 1:33).

Carl Kraeling, an eminent historian and archaeologist who had the unusual privilege of holding the position of department chair in both Near Eastern Languages and New Testament Criticism and

Interpretation while teaching at Yale, appears to have been the first to propose that Jesus raised the ghost of John the Baptist to perform powerful works for him:

> Between demons as the servants of magicians, and spirits of the dead used in a similar way there is no basic distinction. Both are beings of the spiritual order, not limited by time or space, and endowed with supernatural powers... What the people and Herod originally said about Jesus' relation to John was that Jesus was using the spirit of John brought back from the dead to perform his miracles for him.[2]

The gospel of Mark establishes Jesus' reputation as a master manipulator of spirits right at the outset. Jesus teaches "as one who has authority and not like the scribes" (Mark 1:22). Lest a shadow of doubt remain about what Jesus' authority encompasses, Mark has Jesus' Jewish contemporaries answer:

> "What is this? A new teaching based on authority—he gives orders to the unclean spirits and they obey him!" And instantly the report about him spread out in every direction into the whole region of Galilee. (Mark 1:27b-28)

Jesus' fame is clearly linked to exorcism, not to textual acumen—a superior command of the interpretation of Jewish law would hardly be the sort of news that would spread like wildfire among the mostly illiterate country folk of rural Palestine, "this mob that knows nothing of the law" (John 7:49). Jesus is sometimes addressed as "Rabbi," but just what the speakers intended by that title is not clear. In Mark, Jesus is so addressed by Peter, James, and John after they witness the transfiguration (Mark 9:5). In John, Nicodemus calls Jesus Rabbi, but appears to do so in recognition of his miraculous signs (John 3:2).

How could Herod have failed to hear reports about the healer from Nazareth? According to Mark, Jesus quickly established a regional reputation as an accomplished exorcist–"he went through all of Galilee, preaching in their synagogues and casting out devils" (Mark 1:39). After the initial report from Capernaum (Mark 1:21), news that Jesus had returned home caused a dense crowd to gather (Mark 2:1-2). When Jesus left, a mob of Galileans followed, joined by the curious from Judea, Jerusalem, Idumea, villages across the Jordan, and from Tyre and Sidon (Mark 3:7-8).

By then, Jesus has become such a celebrity that he can no longer openly enter a town (Mark 1:45). He instead chooses twelve disciples, sending them out "to preach and to have authority to cast out demons" (Mark 3:14-15).

Jesus' reputation as an exorcist continues to spread; soon other Jewish exorcists begin to invoke the power of his name–"for his name became known" (Mark 6:14). "Jesus of Nazareth" is literally a name to conjure with. "Teacher," said John, "we saw someone driving out demons in your name and we told him to stop, because he is not one of us" (Mark 9:38).

The use of Jesus' name by other exorcists has long been recognized as "an example of professional magical use,"[3] a practice that continued after his death: "Some Jews who went around driving out evil spirits tried to invoke the name of the Lord Jesus over those who were demon-possessed. They would say, 'In the name of the Jesus whom Paul preaches, I command you to come out'" (Acts 19:13). Regarding the unknown exorcist of Mark 9:38, Schäfer notes, "using the powerful name of Jesus had nothing to do with believing in Jesus ... the magical use of the name of Jesus worked automatically, no matter whether or not the magician believed in Jesus."[4] That assessment is supported by a saying attributed to Jesus: "Many will say to me on that day, 'Lord, Lord, did we not prophesy in your name and in your name drive out demons and in your name perform many miracles?'" (Matt. 7:22).

The account of the centurion's slave boy provides further insight into the nature of Jesus' authority over spirits:

> As he entered Capernaum, a centurion came to him, entreating him, "Lord, my boy is lying at home paralyzed, suffering terribly."
>
> Jesus said to him, "I will come and heal him."
>
> The centurion replied, "Lord, I am not worthy for you to step under my roof, but say the word and my boy will be healed. For I, too, am a man with authority, having soldiers under my command, and I say to this one, "Go!" and he goes, and to another, "Come!" and he comes, and to my slave, "Do this!" and he does it." (Matt. 8:5-9)

The wording of the story of the centurion and his boy—"To my slave, 'Do this!' and he does it"—is nearly identical to a spell preserved in the magical papyri in which the magician commands his spirit assistant, "Do this task and he does it immediately."[5] The account in Matthew is also remarkably like a spell in the Jewish spell book, the *Sepher Ha-Razim*: "to rule over spirits and over demons, to send them (wherever you wish) so they will go out like slaves."[6]

After an analysis of the story of the centurion's boy, Jennings and Liew conclude that the centurion

> believes that Jesus can order the coming and going of the demon that has been "torturing" his boy-love with paralysis because he believes that Jesus is the commander or the ruler of that and other demons. In other words, not only are the centurion and the Pharisees in agreement about how authority operates, they further concur on the identity of Jesus as a commanding officer in the chain of demonic beings.[7]

Although one might expect rejoicing from a population freed from the power of Satan by a formidable exorcist, the response to Jesus' power is not relief, but fear. The Pharisees and Herodians begin to plot his murder (Mark 3:6), his family claims Jesus is "out of his mind" (Mark 3:21), and the scribes who come down from Jerusalem to see what all the commotion is about claim that Jesus "has Beelzeboul" and that he casts out demons by the ruler of the demons (Mark 3:22). Jesus' own disciples are terrified of his powers (Mark 4:41). The people of Gerasa, where Jesus casts demons out of a man and allows them to enter a herd of swine, fear him and beg him to leave (Mark 5:15, 17).

That Jesus "has Beelzeboul" is a clear accusation of sorcery. Indeed it is a claim that Jesus is the magician *par excellence* because he has bound Beelzeboul himself, the prince of demons. As Eitrem noted in his classic essay on demonology in the New Testament, "it marks the proper distance between John the Baptist and Jesus when John is said to 'have a demon' (Matt. xi.18) but Jesus is said to 'have Beelzebub' (Mark iii.22)."[8] According to the explanation advanced by his enemies, Jesus is more powerful than John because he controls a more powerful demon, and Jesus himself supports the claim that he has bound Beelzeboul:

> "How can Satan cast out Satan? If a kingdom divides against itself, that kingdom cannot stand, and if a house divides against itself, that house will not be able to stand. So if Satan rises up against himself and becomes divided, he cannot stand. To the contrary, his end has come."
>
> "No one can enter the strong man's house to plunder his possessions unless he first binds the strong man, and then he plunders his house." (Mark 3:23-27)

As promised by John the Baptist, "the one coming after me is stronger than I am" (Matt. 3:11). Jesus has broken into Satan's house and overpowered him–"The seventy-two returned with joy and said, 'Lord, even the demons submit to us in your name.' He replied, 'I saw Satan fall like lightning from heaven'" (Luke 10:17-18). Little wonder the demons ask, "Have you come to destroy us?" (Mark 1:24).

To his credit, Kraeling understood the active meaning of "having Beelzebub":

> This does not mean that Jesus is the unfortunate plaything of Beelzebub; it means, rather, that Jesus is accused of being a magician who by incantations and magical practices has obtained control over Beelzebub and makes him do his bidding even when this is to Beelzebub's own disadvantage.[9]

The belief that magicians drove out one demon with the aid of a yet more powerful demon–"driving out one nail with another"[10] as the satirist Lucian put it–is reflected in the historian Eusebius' claim that the wonder-working Apollonius accomplished a famous exorcism "with the help of a more important demon."[11] An example of "*to have a spirit*" found in Revelation further confirms that "to have Beelzeboul" is to *command* Beelzeboul–the risen Christ is "the one who has the seven spirits of God and the seven stars" (Rev. 3:1).

Hanse says these "seven spirits are thought of as autonomous beings, and they are equated with the seven angels which stand before God." As to what it means for Christ to "have" them, he replies, "It obviously means that He has authority over them, that He can command them."[12]

That the exorcist or sorcerer controls the demon is the whole point of Jesus' question, "How can one enter a strong man's house and seize his belongings *unless one first binds the strong man*?" (Matt. 12:29). After a thorough review of the intrinsic evidence of the gospel accounts, Samain concluded that to "have Beelzeboul" must be understood in an active sense, *to have authority over* the demon:

> Christ is the master of Beelzeboul and he controls him to the point of using him to perform exorcisms ... joined with the ruler of the demons, he compels him, by using his name, to perform the miracles he wants, particularly exorcisms; no spirit, no demonic power, can resist him ... [*Daimonion echei*: "he has a demon"] therefore means that Jesus is a false prophet, a magician.[13]

Samain's conclusion agrees perfectly with the explanation of the Christian apologist Origen, who above all other writers from antiquity provides us with the most detailed account of how exorcism and magic were thought to work: "Once we concede that it is consistent with the existence of magic and sorcery, made active by evil demons that are invoked, *spell-bound by magical charms*, submitting to practitioners of sorcery ..."[14]

According to the early Christian writer Origen–following the "strong man" of Jesus' analogy–demons are *bound*, forced to submit by prayers or incantations, a magical *force majeure*. "This kind can never be cast out except by prayer" (Mark 9:29). In the Christian spiritual economy, that is accomplished by using the powerful name of Jesus: "Did we not cast out demons *in your name*?" (Matt. 7:22).

Apologist scholars frequently say that spells and prayers are different in kind. But their claim is utterly overturned by ancient usage. Spells in the magical papyri that are contemporaneous with early Christianity are often called "prayers" (*euchai*), as they ought to know. Jewish magicians also failed to observe any distinction between spells and prayers; the *Sepher Ha-Razim* instructs the magician, "fall upon your face to the earth and pray this prayer."[15]

According to Origen, the confessions of Christian faith are "just like spells that have been filled with power."[16] Prayers and confessions of faith, like the magic spells they resemble, invoke spirits to act, and what, after all, are incantations used to drive out demons if not prayers to be delivered from evil?

The Greek verb *energeō* and the corresponding noun *energeia*–the source of the English word *energy*–are used in ancient magical texts for working sorcery. *Energeō* "generally refers to the (activated) power of magic... the actual 'activating' of a magic spell."[17] In the New Testament *energeō* is generally used to describe the effects of spirit entities, including demons.[18]

A brief survey of the magical papyri help to contextualize *energeō* and its cognates: "the ritual called 'the Sword,' which is unequaled owing to its *power*,"[19] "the sacred *power* of the symbols you are about to acquire,"[20] "the preparation of the *magical working*,"[21] "pull up the plant while invoking the name of the demon, demanding that it be *very effective* (*energesteros*),"[22] "you have the rite of the greatest and sacred *power* (*energēmatos*)."[23]

Early Christian writings use *energeō* in exactly the same way as the surviving magical spells. Paul's letter to the Ephesians, for example, completely agrees with the broader cultural assumption that *persons raised from the dead are sources of miraculous power*. The Ephesian Christians will know "the surpassing greatness of his power among us who believe, according to *the working* (*tēn energeian*) of the power of his might, which *he put into operation* (*energēsen*) by raising Christ from the dead" (Eph. 1:19-20). The spirit of the risen Christ stands against "the ruler of the authority of the air, the spirit even now *at work* (*energountos*) in the sons of disobedience" (Eph. 2:2).

Ghosts as Magical Assistants

In addition to having a demon as a powerful helper, a magician might also employ a ghost as his assistant, "particularly the spirit of a man who died violently or ghosts of important persons [who] are conceived as locally influential"[24] as this formula from the magical papyri indicates:

> I beseech you, Lord Helios, listen to me [name] and grant me the power over this *spirit of a man killed violently* (*biothanatou pneumatos*) from whose tent I hold [a body part]. I have him with me [name of deceased], a *helper* (*boēthon*), an avenger for whatever business I desire.[25]

The "tent" in question is the body, the house of the soul, in this case a corpse; the identical metaphor occurs in 2 Corinthians where "in the tent" (2 Cor. 5:4) means "in the body." The ghost of the murdered man is the sorcerer's "helper" (*boēthos*), a spirit like the risen Jesus, "the Lord, *my helper* (*emou boēthos*)" (Heb. 13:6).

As a *biaiothanatos*, a victim of violence, John the Baptist has a spirit with the makings of an unquiet ghost "whose power flows simply from the fact that he is dead and angry about it . . . these are potential actors in ghost stories, dangerous and partly wakeful."[26] Diviners and conjurers enlisted the souls of the violently slain, "part of a wider class of the restless dead, who came to be thought of as the typical instruments of malign magic."[27]

"As syncretistic magic developed, sorcerers came to think of infants, young unmarried adults, dead gladiators, executed criminals, and other victims of violent deaths as constituting a pool of the dispossessed upon whom it was possible to call as involuntary helpers," notes Nock. The "unwed and the childless constitute an important subsection of the *ahori*; neither group possesses any progeny to render them the customary honors after death."[28] Or as Aubert phrases it, the ghosts of those who died of "unnatural causes" or lacked proper burial, particularly those who died on the cross or on the gallows, "had the right profile for the job."[29]

Accordingly, the writings of Luke and Paul everywhere presuppose that Jesus' power (*dunamis*) is derived from his violent death by crucifixion. The apostles testify to Jesus' resurrection "with *great power*" (Acts 4:33). As Kraeling observed, *dunameis* "are either 'mighty works' (cf. Mk 6 5) or the powers by which such works are done (cf. in Mk 5 30)."[30]

The gospel writers' view of a connection between violent death and resulting power is now widely recognized by specialists in New Testament studies. If *dunamis* "is understood here as 'miracle working power,' that is, the sort of power that works [*dunameis*] ('miracles'), then the apostles' role in testifying to the resurrection is not just oral, but linked directly to their miracle working."[31] The raising of Jesus "is the foundation miracle for the whole narrative of Acts"[32] as it is in the gospel of John, which specifies that the spirit will not be given until Jesus is "glorified" (John 7:39). In Acts, the "miracles, wonders and signs, which God did among you through" Jesus (2:2), are consistently linked to the power of the risen Jesus, "nailed up and killed by the hands of lawless men" (2:23, 33).

The gospel of Mark shares the basic assumption behind necromancy: *as residents of the spirit world, ghosts and demons know both the future and truths concealed from mortals.* A voice from heaven first announces that Jesus is the Son of God (Mark 1:11) but the next spirit that identifies Jesus as the "holy one" is a demon (1:24). The demons "knew who he was" (1:34) and are blabbering it everywhere—Jesus is the "Son of God" (3:11). The Gerasene demoniac, who "lived among the tombs" (5:3), implying possession by ghosts, identifies Jesus as the "Son of the Most High God" (5:7).

Jesus the Necromancer

Nock calls necromancy "the practice or art of obtaining information concerning the future by communication with the dead who ... are thought to share with gods and demons a knowledge of things beyond the ken of living mortals." The term "describes the practice of accomplishing through the instrumentality of the spirits of the dead any or all deeds belonging to the sphere of 'black magic.'"[33] That, observes Peter Bolt about

Mark 6:14-16, is just what Herod thought Jesus was doing; he "considered Jesus to be a magician who had raised John's spirit in order to capitalize on its power." And now we understand the focus on John's beheading:

> A beheaded man, as a [*biaiothanatos*], would make a powerful ghost and would be highly sought after by the magicians. When Herod suggests that Jesus has "raised" John, he uses language that regularly appears in the magical material for the summoning of the ghostly *daimon* from its rest in the underworld in order to do the magician's bidding.[34]

Although the modern rationalist might suppose a *headless* spirit would be worse than useless, the magical papyri contain frequent references to the power of headless entities of various sorts.[35] Nevertheless, "the most common measure for ridding the living of a revenant was decapitation"[36] and Kraemer has proposed that Mark emphasized the method of John's execution specifically to counter a rumor that Jesus was John raised from the dead:

> *Why is Jesus not John resurrected from the dead?* The gospel narratives are clear that this identification has been suggested. It would seem to be troubling to followers of Jesus for obvious reasons, namely, that it obscures distinctions between Jesus and John and may even subordinate the former to the latter . . . Jesus is not John raised from the dead because John's body and head were severed: only his body was buried by his disciples, while the whereabouts of his head, given to Herodias, are unknown, thus, implicitly, making his bodily resurrection impossible.[37]

The mutilation of corpses to prevent the emergence of wrathful ghosts is widely attested, "rendering the ghost powerless through some direct effect which mutilation of the body would have upon the shade."[38] *Maschalismos* or "armpitting," removing the limbs from a murdered corpse and stringing them together in a gruesome necklace suspended around the torso, supposedly deprived the ghost of the power to avenge itself by literally disarming the potentially vengeful spirit. David responds to the assassination of Ishbosheth, a son of Saul, by ordering his men to kill the assassins–"They cut off their hands and feet and hung the bodies by the pool in Hebron" (2 Sam. 4:12). Their post-mortem mutilation may reflect poetic retribution for the deeds done by the assassins' hands and their travel with the severed head of their victim as proof of their deed, or it may have been a measure "to avert the possibility of revenge"[39] by the murderer's ghosts.

Christianity likewise took a number of precautions to keep ghosts from haunting, the "stake and, later, holy water were to prevent the deceased from leaving the grave."[40] During the Middle Ages, corpse mutilation, which could include staking, burning of the corpse, and decapitation was thought to prevent vampirism, "that wildest and ghastliest of superstitions."[41]

Why would Jesus have selected the ghost of John as a source of power? This observation by Daniel Ogden suggests the answer: "Often the prime criterion for selecting a ghost for necromancy was the relevance of the individual ghost to the matter at hand. Hence, the ghost exploited was often a dear one . . . A further category that may have been particularly valued for necromancy was that of the exalted ghost."[42] Who could have been more relevant to Jesus' career than John the Baptist? He is Jesus' forerunner, "the voice crying out in the wilderness" (John 1:23), even a relative according to Luke (Luke 1:36), and of those born of woman, who was greater than John? (Matt. 11:11).

Comparing Mark's account with those of the other gospels suggests that Kraeling was spot on. The report of Herod's opinion in Mark, which at the very least implies that he considered Jesus to be a necromancer, has been substantially re-written by Matthew and Luke. Kannaday notes that the "text of the New Testament was in a potential sense an ammunition magazine, a common store of gunpowder and musket balls critical to victory in the campaign being waged by both pagan intellectuals and apologetic defenders."**43** The writers of the other Synoptics attempt to preserve the tradition about John the Baptist while at the same time disarming it, removing its explosive claim about the source of Jesus' powers.

In the process of editing his version of Mark's story, Matthew has Herod say, "This man is John the Baptist. He was raised from the dead and that is why the *powers are working in* (*energousin*) him" (Matt. 14:2). The text of Matthew has Herod simply identify Jesus as John raised from the dead, but this clumsy rewriting does not address the question of why "the powers" would be working in someone raised from the dead–"there is no evidence of a contemporary expectation that the resurrected dead would be endowed with miraculous powers they did not possess during their lifetimes."**44** And as David Aune observes, "it is unclear how a resurrected John could be thought to perform miracles when he had not done so previous to his execution."**45** On the other hand, the angry ghost of a man unjustly executed is another matter entirely.

Even more obviously, Matthew's reworking of Mark fails to address how Herod could have confused Jesus, who was still very much alive and whose "name" was widely recognized, with John the Baptist, the man whose execution he had just ordered. If, as the gospels assert, John performed no powerful works while still alive (John 10:41) even though "he will go before [Jesus] *in the spirit and power* of Elijah" (Luke 1:17), a prophet of exceptional miracle-working power, how could Herod have imagined that John would start to produce a whole gasp-inducing series of wonders once raised from the dead? As Kraeling noted, identifying Jesus with John "fails to take into account the strong individuality of John and the difference between him and Jesus."**46**

That Matthew's retelling of the story contains an apologetic intention is suggested by his stipulation that John's disciples come to recover his now headless body, bury it, and tell Jesus about it

(Matt. 14:12-13). Matthew may have wanted to reassure his readers that John is not an *ataphos*, an unburied man likely to become a restless spirit. Kraeling:

> It was commonly believed in ancient times that there were two classes of spirits of the dead which were relatively easy to conjure up and were thus most accessible for the purposes of "black magic." The first class was that of the [*ataphoi*], spirits of persons who had not received a regular burial... The second class, relatively more numerous and less immediately attached to a specific locality, is that of the [*biaiothanatoi*], spirits of persons who had died a violent death.[47]

Luke, on the other hand, takes a different approach—he produces a Herod who is "completely perplexed" (Luke 9:7-9), unable even to begin to explain Jesus' famous powers. Garrett admits that Luke has rephrased "the most damaging part of the account" to avoid the charge of necromancy, but next claims that the evangelists "did not share modern readers' frequent assumptions that identity of appearance implies actual identity."[48] Garrett does not explain how she knows what assumptions the anonymous evangelists shared; if their own opinion is to be allowed, it would seem that appearances and identity were tightly linked, that "trees are known by their fruit" (Matt. 7:20).

The alterations and omissions of potentially incriminating details by Matthew and Luke indicate the writers shared some assumptions about appearance and identity—why emphasize Jesus' exorcisms unless the performances established his identity, that Jesus is the Son of God? (Luke 4:41). Garrett's claim also ignores the reputation of Jews among gentiles; gentiles such as Lucian regarded the Jews as accomplished exorcists and Jesus the Jew as a magician.

> Everyone knows about the Syrian from Palestine,[49] the master of his craft, and how he receives many

moonstruck, frothing at the mouth and eyes rolling, and he sets them aright and sends them away sound of mind . . . standing beside them as they lie there, he asks from whence [the demons] have come into the body. The madman himself is silent, but the demon answers in Greek or a barbarian tongue from whence and how he entered the man. By adjuring, or if the spirit does not obey, threatening, he drives out the demon.[50]

Elsewhere Lucian refers to Jesus as "that crucified trickster,"[51] and that he intended to parody the claims of the gospel of Matthew is easy to suspect given his examples of those who die violently:

"We are just attempting to persuade this hard-headed fellow," Eucrates said, pointing at me, "to believe that some spirits and ghosts and souls of dead men exist and wander around above ground and appear to whomever they wish." I blushed and bowed my head out of respect for Arignotus.

"Perhaps, Eucrates," he said, "Tychiades means to say that only the souls to those who died by violence walk about, for example if someone hanged himself,[52] or was beheaded,[53] or crucified[54] or departed life in similar fashion, but that those who die from the usual causes do not."[55]

Lucian may have had Jesus himself in mind when he composed his story of the Syrian from Palestine. Were he and his audiences enjoying a joke at Christian expense? Lucian's reference to Jesus as the "crucified trickster" "enraged pious scholiasts who saw it as yet another of Lucian's blasphemies."[56] Regarding the exorcism tale, Morton Smith said, "It is possible this parody was inspired by some gospel story."[57] Among pagans, Jesus' fame for magic was such that many early apologists such as Irenaeus, Origen, Arnobius, Justin Martyr, and Lactantius, found themselves defending him from the accusation.[58]

It will come as little surprise that Kraeling's claims have received short shrift among New Testament scholars with an apologetic bent—Twelftree[59] and Hoehner[60] relegate Kraeling to the endnotes and neither addresses his thesis in any detail. Notwithstanding, several lines of evidence converge to support Kraeling's reading of the text: Both John and Jesus, were well known—"People went out to [John] from Jerusalem and all Judea and the whole region of the Jordan" (Matt. 3:5)—and their careers overlapped. Herod could not have confused them. Therefore Matthew's identification of Jesus as John back from the dead fails on textual grounds and is historically impossible, the type of mistake only an author who was not an eyewitness could make.

The source of Jesus' authority over demons became a topic of speculation; some "were saying, 'John the Baptist has been raised from the dead *and because of this the powers are at work* in [Jesus]'" (Mark 6:14). The language of the common people match the terminology of the magical papyri word for word. The papyri remain our clearest window into folk belief about magicians who raised ghosts as magical assistants.

In fact, the critics of early Christianity often compare Christian exorcism to "the works of sorcerers" and street magicians "who drive demons out of men, and blow away diseases, and call up the souls of the heroes."[61] Given the abundance of testimony from ancient sources, Kraeling's explanation has far more support than the conspicuously improbable alternatives proposed by Matthew and Luke.

That the notion of raising a ghost for magical purposes would never have suggested itself in the context of early Christianity is questionable. Besides references to the practice in near-contemporary non-Christian sources, the *Homilies* of the early 4th century contain a reference to just such a ritual attributed to the infamous Simon: "For he set out to commit murder, as he revealed as a friend among friends, extracting the soul of a boy from his own body by means of abominable invocations, a helper to cause the appearance of whatever he pleased."[62]

Kraeling's careful attention to the text distinguished "what *the people* were saying about Jesus"[63] and Herod's own conclusion. "Some claimed Jesus' miraculous powers could be attributed to the 'raising' of John "and because of this the powers are at work in [Jesus] but *others* were saying, 'He's Elijah'"—not an impossible conclusion if Elijah was expected to return[64]. Yet *others* "were saying, 'A prophet like one of the prophets.'" (Mark 6:14-15) "But when Herod heard, he said, 'John, the one I beheaded, *this one* has been raised'" (Mark 6:16).

Herod's answer, "this one," strongly implies his rejection of the other possibilities: Jesus is not Elijah, nor is he a prophet "like one of the prophets." Jesus has "raised" or "awakened" the ghost of John and "because of this the powers are at work in him." Herod's response, "this one (*houtos*)" serves both to identify the "risen" John as the source of Jesus' power and to dismiss the alternative theories. The demonstrative, "this one," serves a similar purpose elsewhere in Mark: "*This* [and no other] is my Son, the beloved . . ." (Mark 9:7)[65]

Since Kraeling wrote, substantial progress has been made in understanding the popular culture of the Greco-Roman world as it applies to early Christianity. We understand it now as a culture obsessed with magic and the supernatural.

With the publication of material collected and edited by Mordecai Morgalioth,[66] it has become increasingly obvious that popular Jewish culture was likewise preoccupied with magic. The broader understanding of the society in which Jesus and his first followers moved both supports Kraeling's interpretation of Mark 6:14-16 and clarifies the apologetic intentions of Matthew and Luke who appear to have understood all too well the implications of the text as it stands in Mark.

Notes

1. Oscar Gustav Rejlander, 1855.

2. Kraeling, *Journal of Biblical Literature* 59 (1940) 154-55.

3. Hull, *Hellenistic Magic and the Synoptic Tradition*, 72.

4. Schäfer, *Jesus in the Talmud*, 60.

5. Preisendanz, op. cit., I, 182.

6. Morgan, op. cit., 18.

7. Jennings & Liew, *Journal of Biblical Literature* 124 (2004) 486.

8. Eitrem, *Some Notes on the Demonology in the New Testament*, 4.

9. Kraeling, op. cit, 154.

10. Harmon, *Lucian* III, 335.

11. Conybeare, *The Life of Apollonius of Tyana* II, 551, 567.

12. Hanse, *The Theological Dictionary of the New Testament* II, 821.

13. Samain, *Ephemerides Theologicae Lovanienses* 15 (1932) 468, 470, 482.

    My translation of "... le Christ est maitre de Béelzéboul et le domine au point d l'employer pour opérer ses exorcismes... uni au chef des demons, il le forcerait, possédant son nom, à opérer les prodiges qu'il veut et specialment les exorcismes; nul esprit, nulle puissance démoniaque ne lui résiste-...[*Daimonion echei*] signifie donc encore que Jésus est un faux profète magicien."

14. Origen, *Contra Celsum* II, 51.

15. Morgan, op. cit., 71.

16. Origen, op. cit., III, 68.

17. Kotansky, *Greek Magical Amulets*, 241.

18. Bertram, *Theological Dictionary of the New Testament*, II, 653.

19. Preisendanz, op. cit., IV, 1718.

20. Ibid, I, 274.

21. Ibid, III, 290.

22. Ibid, IV, 2976.

23. Ibid, XII, 317.

24. Harrison, *Journal of Hellenic Studies* 19 (1899) 205.

25. Preisendanz, op. cit., IV, 1947-54.

    The spirit of the prematurely dead is "restless and discontented, aggrieved because he has lost part of the life on earth to which he was entitled...[premature death] sends him into the other world still a vigorous spirit, who has not used up the energy he would otherwise have spent in living in the body... if a potent spirit of this kind could be pressed into the service of an expert, it would prove a valuable familiar or an energetic subordinate." H. Rose, "Ghost Ritual in Aeschylus," *Harvard Theological Review* 43 (1950) 271.

26. Vermeule, *Aspects of Death in Early Greek Art and Poetry*, 27.

    In reference to the ghosts of *heroes*, those whose lives were marked by unusual achievement, Johnston remarks, "Like other *biaiothanatoi*, these angry souls were dangerous and might have to be appeased. But, having led extraordinary lives, they lead extraordinary deaths as well, possessing powers either to aid or injure the living beyond those of the normal *biaiothanatoi* . . ." *Restless Dead*, 153.

27. Gordon, op. cit., 176.

28. Nock, *Vigiliae Christianae* 4 (1950) 135, 138.

    "No less dreaded is the anger of those who have not met with a natural death, the biaiothantoi . . . The one 'killed in battle' and the unburied 'who lies in the wilderness without the covering of earth' . . . These are the critical, dangerous cases, somebody 'killed in battle' or else unburied and hence restlessly wandering about. Burkert, *The Orientalizing Revolution*, 66.

29. Aubert, *Greek, Roman, and Byzantine Studies* 30 (1989) 437.

30. Kraeling, op. cit., 149.

31. Reimer, *Miracle and Magic*, 91.

32. Myllykoski, *Wonders Never Cease*, 162.

33. Kraeling, op. cit., 147.

34. Bolt, *Jesus' Defeat of Death: Persuading Mark's Early Readers*, 191-92.

35. Preisendanz, op. cit., II, 11; IV, 2132; V, 98, 125, 130, 145; VII, 233, 243, 442, VIII, 91.

36. Lecouteux, op. cit., 141.

37. Kraemer, *Journal of Biblical Literature* 125 (2006) 343.

38. Kittredge, op. cit., 154.

39. Bloch-Smith, op. cit., 221.

40. Lecouteux, op. cit., 39.

41. Kittredge, op. cit., 165-166.

42. Ogden, *Greek and Roman Necromancy*, 226-27.

43. Kannaday, *Apologetic Discourse and the Scribal Tradition*, 21.

44. Frayer-Griggs, *Matthew and Mark Across Perspectives*, 40.

45. Aune, *Aufstieg und Niedergang der römischen Welt* 2.23.2, 1542.

46. Kraeling, op. cit., 153.

II: THE GHOST OF JOHN THE BAPTIST   51

47. Kraeling, op. cit., 154-55.

48. Garrett, *The Demise of the Devil*, 3.

49. "The context of Lucian's tale is Judaeo-Christian. The term 'Syrian from Palestine' in effect means 'Jewish.'" Ogden, *In Search of the Sorcerer's Apprentice*, 133.

50. Lucian, *The Lover of Lies*, 16 (my translation).

51. Lucian, *On the Death of Peregrinus*, 13 (my translation).

52. Matthew 27:5.

53. Matthew 14:10.

54. Matthew 27:35, 38.

55. Lucian, *Lover of Lies*, 29 (my translation).

56. Jones, *Culture and Society in Lucian*, 48.

57. Smith, *Jesus the Magician*, 57.

58. Ricks, *Ancient Magic and Ritual Power*, 141.

59. Twelftree, *Jesus the Exorcist*, 208.

60. Hoehner, *Herod Antipas*, 188.

61. Origen, op. cit., I, 68.

62. Roberts & Donaldson, *Ante-Nicene Christian Library*, XVII, 44.

63. Kraeling, op. cit., 148. (The emphasis is Kraeling's.)

64. Malachi 3:23-24 is often cited to support the notion that Elijah would appear before the coming of the Messiah, but as Faierstein notes, "There is no reference in these verses to the Messiah ... Moreover, there is no evidence that these verses were understood in any ancient source to imply a relationship between Elijah and the Messiah ... contrary to the accepted scholarly consensus, almost no evidence has been preserved which indicates that the concept of Elijah as forerunner of the Messiah was widely known or accepted in the first century C.E." *Journal of Biblical Literature* 100 (1981) 77, 86.

65. On the particularizing use of *houtos* see Baur, Arndt & Gingrich, *A Greek-English Lexicon of the New Testament*, 600-601.

66. Margolioth, *Sepher Ha-Razim*, 1966, Yediot Achronot.

III

An Abundance of Visions

> Religious mysticism is only one half of mysticism. The other half has no accumulated traditions except which the textbooks on insanity supply.
>
> —William James, *The Varieties of Religious Experience*, 1902.

The people of the past, like the people of the present, held many incompatible beliefs about death and the dead. "Like water spilled on the ground, which cannot be recovered, so we must die" (2 Sam. 14:14). "Surely the fate of human beings is like that of the animals; the same fate awaits them both: As one dies, so dies the other. All have the same breath; humans have no advantage over animals. Everything is meaningless. All go to the same place; all come from dust, and to dust all return. Who knows if the human spirit rises upward and if the spirit of the animal goes down into the earth?" (Eccl. 3:19-21). *And yet*: "But your dead will live, Lord; their bodies will rise—let those who dwell in the dust wake up and shout for joy" (Isa. 26:19). *Or*, "Multitudes who sleep in the dust of the earth will awake: some to everlasting life, others to shame and everlasting contempt" (Dan. 12:2).

Families were buried together; "gathered to one's fathers"[1] was not simply a figure of speech. Denial of proper burial could involve refusal of interment with family members—"your body will not be buried in the tomb of your ancestors" (1 Kings 13:22)—or at worst exposure of the corpse to be consumed by animals as in the case of Jezebel: "dogs will devour her on the plot of ground at Jezreel, and no one will bury her" (2 Kings 9:10). Likewise, the Zealot faction murdered Anan, the High Priest, as well as Jesus ben Gamla in Jerusalem during the first Jewish-Roman war (66-73 CE), and tossed their naked corpses over the wall to be eaten by dogs.[2]

All around the ancient Mediterranean, the "political and social fabric" was sustained in part by "a common burial plot on [the family's] ancestral lands."[3] To neglect the burial of the dead—"Let the dead bury their own dead, but you go and proclaim the kingdom of God" (Luke 9:60)–signals intent to disrupt the basis of the social order.

In popular belief, the dead could be consulted through mediums (Isa. 8:19) or through *incubation*, sleeping on or near tombs in order to contact spirits in dreams, the likely reference to Israelites "who sit in tombs, and spend the night in secret places" (Isa. 65:4). Of course, that all presupposes that the dead are conscious, able to communicate with and appear to the living, and connected in some way to their graves.

In the most famous case of biblical necromancy, the risen Samuel appears *only to the medium*. Saul asks, "What do you see?" and the medium replies, "I see a ghostly figure coming up out of the earth." Saul then asks, "What does he look like?" and only after the medium describes the ghost does Saul recognize that it's Samuel (1 Sam. 38:13-14).

Jesus' post-mortem appearances fall into three general categories, *visions*, *epiphanies*, and *apparitions*, but the distinctions are not always clear nor are the details completely consistent. For example, the account of Jesus' appearance to Paul on the road to Damascus is reported in three places in Acts.

A Bacchic Vision of Jesus?

The story differs in detail with each retelling, but despite its occurrence *after* Jesus' resurrection, it's not typically offered as a post-resurrection apparition *per se*. According to the first report, Paul falls to the ground while the men with him stand speechless, hearing a sound but seeing no one (Acts 9:7-8). In the second version, Paul's traveling companions see the light (Acts 22:9) and in the third version of the story all the men fall to the ground (Acts 26:14).

In an utterly bizarre twist, the voice of Jesus, "speaking to [Paul] in *Aramaic*," quotes the *Greek text of the Bacchae* nearly verbatim: "It is hard for you to kick against the goads" (Acts 26:14).

And that's not the only feature the Road to Damascus story shares with the *Bacchae*. Not by a long shot.

"Divine intervention is sudden (*Bacchae* 576, *Acts* 9.3, 22.6). The group hears the voice of the god but does not see him (*Bacchae* 576-95, *Acts* 9.7). To the lightning in *Bacchae* corresponds the description of the light appearing to Saul in terms of lightning (9.3, 22.6). The Dionysiac chorus falls to the ground and Pentheus collapses, and Saul falls to the ground (as does also, at 26.14, the group that accompanies him). The command to rise up ... is given by Dionysus to the chorus and by the Lord to Saul." Seaford concludes, "These similarities are too numerous to be coincidental."[4]

If, in fact, the account of Paul's conversion has been 'fleshed out' with material cribbed from the *Bacchae*, it supports our contention that the gospel writers were willing and able to plagiarize material from the broader Greco-Roman culture in addition to using material appropriated from the Hebrew scriptures.

Soon after his conversion, Saul, aka Paul, sees Jesus again, but under different circumstances.

> It happened that after returning to Jerusalem, while I was praying in the temple, I fell into a state of ecstasy and I saw him saying to me, "Hurry and leave Jerusalem at once because they will not accept your testimony about me." (Acts 22:17-18)

Jesus' appearance to Paul in the temple is an ecstatic vision, but his manifestation on the road to Damascus has the characteristics of other epiphanies: light, voices, glowing raiment (Matt. 28:3; Luke 24:3), supernatural entities, and natural upheavals (Matt. 28:2 5). Visions during prayer were known (Dan. 9:20). And, Strelan notes,

> That [Paul's] prayer included an ecstatic vision is not at all unusual ... it is quite likely that Temple prayer had

rhythm and repetitive elements. In addition, it is possible that the body moved in harmony with the rhythm of the prayer. Such a method of praying is often mantra-like and can induce a hypnotic, ecstatic state.[5]

A trance-like altered state of consciousness was likely associated with Paul's vision; Peter also has a vision while in a state of ecstasy (Acts 10:10-11). And that brings us to the subject of Paul specifically and visions of the dead generally.

The Stigmatic and His Visions

It's not often appreciated that Paul claimed to have *stigmata*, special marks on his body, which demonstrated "the depth of his self-identification with the sufferings of Jesus on the cross"[6]–"for I bear on my body *the marks of Jesus* (*ta stigmata tou Iēsou*)" (Gal. 6:17). It would also appear that Paul self-identified with Old Testament prophets, particularly Jeremiah. Like Jeremiah–"before you were born I set you apart, I appointed you as a prophet to the nations" (Jer. 1:5)–Paul claims that God "set me apart from my mother's womb and called me by his grace . . . so that I might preach [his Son] among the Gentiles" (Gal. 1:15-16).

Paul's sense of special election results in an admittedly idiosyncratic interpretation of Jesus' death and resurrection–Paul clearly states that after Jesus was "revealed" to him, he did not "consult with any man" nor did he travel to Jerusalem to meet the apostles. Instead, he went to Arabia, then to Damascus, and only three years later did he meet for two weeks with Peter and James (Gal. 1:16-19). Fourteen years after that, Paul again went to Jerusalem "in response to a revelation," and met with the "pillars" of the mother church but the meeting "*added nothing*" to his preaching (Gal. 2:2, 6).

In short, Paul "had received [his gospel] directly from God and thus [it] did not conform to any existing tradition," making him "the protagonist of an interpretation of Christianity which had little interest in the career of the historical Jesus."[7] Was Paul's primary motive in reporting his visions to establish proof of the resurrection or to legitimize "his own credentials as an apostle" as well as "the validity of his particular version of the Christian gospel"?[8]

What Paul's visions clearly do is validate his apostolic authority and support his distinctive theology as well. "Am I not an apostle?" he asks. "Have I not seen Jesus our Lord?" (1 Cor. 9:1). God, he reports, was pleased "to *reveal his Son in me* so that I might preach him among the Gentiles" (Gal. 1:15-16). Paul's visions and ecstatic transports establish his apostolic office "in a special limited sense" on a equal footing with Peter, James, "and the other apostles who were called directly by Christ."[9]

A "psychological mechanism" proposed for the post-resurrection visions might very well have applied to Paul: "A conflict between one orientation of faith and a new one goes on below the threshold of consciousness until there is a psychical explosion objectified in a vision with a new conviction taking possession of consciousness."[10]

The Last Trumpet

As we can see from Paul's letters, he taught his converts that they were living at the end of history. The end was so close at hand that the unmarried should not seek to be married and those already married should live as if celibate–"the time is short. From now on those who have wives should live as if they do not" (1 Cor. 7:29). The Thessalonians expected to witness the very End, *alive in the flesh*, "spirit, soul, *and body* ... blameless at the coming of our Lord Jesus Christ" (1 Thess. 5:23).

Paul assured the believers, falsely it turned out, "We will not all sleep, but *we will all be changed*–in a flash, in the twinkling of an eye, at the last trumpet. For the trumpet will sound, the dead will be raised imperishable, and *we will be changed*" (1 Cor. 15:51-52).

Oops. It has long been recognized in mainstream New Testament studies that

> the death of some of their number found the Thessalonian Christians unprepared. Their newly-acquired faith carried with it the expectation of the imminent coming of Jesus, and did not allow for the death of any of their members before this event should take place.[11]

Many studies of the culture of early Christianity have noted the "eschatological fervor of the primitive church and the well-attested presence of manifold ecstatic phenomena among the Christians."[12]

If a modern religious figure made similar claims–to bear the marks of Christ on his body, to have been designated by God even before birth, to have received personal revelations–or preached that believers presently alive would not die but be suddenly transformed–he would very likely be marked down as delusional. Some who met Paul in person did exactly that.

"While Paul was saying this in his defense, Festus said in a loud voice, 'Paul, you are out of your mind!'" (Acts 26:24). In point of fact, Paul reminded members of his own house churches that their behavior would appear insane to outsiders: "If the whole church comes together and everyone speaks in tongues, and inquirers or unbelievers come in, will they not say that you are out of your mind?" (1 Cor. 14:23).

To the skeptic–ancient or modern–Paul's claim that God called him while still in his mother's womb sounds like a delusion of grandeur and his claim to visions and revelations sounds suspiciously like hallucination. In a "comparison of mysticism and psychosis" some investigators have concluded that "hallucinations and grandiose and paranoid delusions did not distinguish the psychotic from the mystic."[13]

Regarding the Montanist or New Prophecy movement of the mid-2nd century, Wypustek states, "Pneumatic inspiration, mediumistic enhancements and prophetic trances were experienced not only by Montanus and his prophetesses" but also other "seers and visionaries." Both pagans and orthodox Christians alike regarded "Montanist ecstasy as resembling madness"[14] and suspiciously like magic.

As Jackson observes, "deeply cherished beliefs are potentially at stake" in the debate over the relationship between religion and mental disease. So "it is perhaps not surprising that the question of the extent of correspondence and distinguishability of psychotic and spiritual experience is largely unresolved."[15] Indeed, the practical difference between *paranormal, superstitious, magical,* and *supernatural* has been called into question and if "magical beliefs were defined as breaking scientific laws of causality,"[16] then by definition the Immaculate Conception and transubstantiation are clearly *magical.* A recent study on the terminology of preternatural experience concluded there are "no essential reasons to set the concepts paranormal, magical, superstitious, and supernatural apart."[17]

Paul claimed repeatedly to have received (presumably) visual communications from Jesus after Jesus died–"Three times I pleaded with the Lord to take it away from me. But he said to me, 'My grace is sufficient for you, for my power is made perfect in weakness'" (2 Cor. 12:8-9). Since "the connection between religiousness and psychosis have been verified historically"[18], it's worth considering what is currently understood about seeing and hearing the recently dead as well as what research into the origins of "spiritual technologies" such as visions, soul flight, and other altered states of consciousness can tell us.

Visions or Hallucinations?

A complex of personality disorders that includes "hyperreligiosity, and hypergraphia–the tendency toward excessive and compulsive writing,"[19] known in the literature of psychology as *Gastaut-Geschwind syndrome*, has been linked in some subjects to temporal lobe epilepsy. The connection between ghosts and insanity, epilepsy, or *morbus caducus*, and possession, "made ill by apparitions," is ancient.[20]

Belief in the paranormal and experiences of seeing or otherwise sensing the dead have been studied extensively and have been found to be surprisingly common. In one study, fifty percent of widowers and forty-six percent of widows "reported hallucinatory experiences of their dead spouses in a clearly waking state."[21] The second most frequent experience after visual apparitions involved "the feeling of an invisible presence" but in some cases the "percipient ... awakened to see an apparition which then vanished or walked through the wall of the room."[22] Consistent with extensively documented ancient beliefs, "another prominent feature was how many [of those seen] ... had suffered violent deaths." Even more striking, "in forty-three cases another person was reported to have been present" during encounters with the dead and "in about one-third of these instances it was reported that the other person had shared the interviewee's experience."[23] Vincent reports that in a study of hundreds of "mystical" experiences, "2.5% involved multiple witnesses."[24]

An increasingly popular explanation for Jesus' apparitions follows from these insights: Jesus sightings then and now are "after-death communications," consistent in detail with "modern-day accounts by non-psychotic individuals."[25] Indeed, Vincent flatly denies that the idea of a physical resurrection was ever entertained by Paul: "Paul knew nothing about a physical resurrection of Jesus ... In reality, the empty tomb adds nothing, as no one saw Jesus revive and walk out of the tomb."[26]

Regardless of how the ancients explained them, there is nothing particularly out of the ordinary about the appearance of ghosts to family members of the deceased. The ghost of Elysios' beloved son appears to him in a dream, which is not difficult to account for "since after all it amounts to no more than this, that a man in deep sorrow performed certain rites in the efficacy of which he believed, and afterwards had a dream which comforted him."[27]

As noted in the Introduction, the world of the New Testament in which the dead are very much present is a "culturally constructed reality" quite different from our own. It's also a world in which visionary experience is neither uncommon nor subject to intense scrutiny. As Craffert observes,

> While not a single text claims that any of the first followers have witnessed Jesus' resurrection, all the available evidence suggests that they were fully convinced about Jesus' resurrection based on visionary experiences... In these visions it is not only Jesus but also other beings or entities (angels or men in white garments) whom they encounter.[28]

But we are no longer living in the "culturally constructed reality" of the New Testament world; in our culture there are naturalistic explanations for visionary experiences, specifically seizures and other physiologic circumstances as possible "biological bases for ecstatic and mystical states."[29] In any case, it nearly goes without saying that visions are culturally determined; the French see visions of Joan of Arc, the British see visions of Saint George, Portuguese schoolgirls see the Virgin Mary, and indigenous peoples see spirits appropriate to their cultures. In short, beliefs about supernatural agency lay downstream from deeply held cultural assumptions and personal psychology.

One naturalistic explanation invokes "temporal lobe transients" or "TLT's," "electrical microseizures without any obvious motor components"[30] such as facial tics or seizures. Such transient events would be "easily accommodated into experience" and would include a range of perceived phenomena ranging from "rushing sounds,"[31] the voice of God or of a spirit, "egocentric references," "divine guidance," and "the special personal significance of chance events,"[32] i.e., omens or "signs." All are consistent with experiences reported in the New Testament.

Interestingly, such microseizures might be triggered or "kindled" by a "specific environmental context (church versus public space)," the smell of incense, "vestibular (rocking) stimuli" such as the back-and-forth motion often observed during prayer, or low blood sugar due to fasting. Persinger characterizes "the loss of a loved one" as one of the most "notorious biochemical disruptors that particularly influence TLT probability," resulting in hallucinations that "appear extraordinarily real and very personal."[33]

That seeing spirits might be "kindled" by the environment is suggested by Frankfurter's observation that sermons about the saints were accompanied by "clouds of incense and the dim light of oil lamps" through which "the martyr's spirit would become tangible to those crowded inside [the church]."[34] "When the gods cause illness and madness, what they do is disrupt the person, and they do so with smells, sounds, sight, *ponoi*, and the like."[35] *Ponoi*, the plural of *ponos*, include physical and mental suffering, fatigue and anxiety.[36]

It's also well known that techniques such as drumming and dancing are used worldwide in shamanic rituals. Such "auditory driving" may trigger "trance states," out-of-body ascents, and "soul flight."[37] It is essential to understand that these are *techniques* often largely under the "volitional control of the practitioner,"[38] who "can voluntarily enter altered states of consciousness," and "experience themselves leaving their bodies and journeying to other realms . . . as a means of acquiring knowledge."[39] Sixty-three percent out of 488 "societies surveyed worldwide use rituals to evoke hallucinations for inspiration or guidance."[40]

While "psychical and mystical experiences are spontaneous," generally speaking, it is also possible that "one can create conditions that set the stage for the experiences."[41] Although paranormal phenomena are often triggered by crisis and emotional distress, the repeated observation that such episodes can also be staged, "kindled," or voluntarily induced by visual or auditory cues, suggests to some investigators that the barrier between the subconscious and conscious is thinner in some subjects. Known as *transliminality*,[42] a porous boundary between the conscious and the subconscious creates a predisposition to creativity, magical thinking, and experience of the paranormal,[43] including "encounters with beings and entities such as angels and the dead."[44]

One ancient possession technology is suggested by this passage from the Old Testament: "As you approach the town, you will meet a procession of prophets coming down from the high place with *lyres, timbrels, pipes and harps* being played before them, and they will be prophesying. The *Spirit of the Lord will come powerfully upon you*, and you will prophesy with them; *and you will be changed into a different person*" (1 Sam. 10:5-6).[45] A very similar technique of inducing an altered state of mind is probably what's described in this passage: "While the harpist was playing, the hand of the Lord came on Elisha" (2 Kings 3:15).

"In Eastern cultures, methods for altering consciousness are embedded in religion."[46] The nature of the altered state of mind is clear from related texts: "three times a prophet is spoken of as *mešuggā*."[47] Those fortunate enough to have some Yiddish will recognize this as "meshugga," a frequently useful word that means "crazy." The connection between prophets and madmen stands confirmed from the context of the Hebrew scriptures—"you should put any maniac who acts like a prophet into the stocks and neck-irons" (Jer. 29:26). The Jewish Hellenist Philo of Alexandria described the process of possession as loss of mind:

> Whenever [the light of the mind] dims, ecstasy and possession naturally assail us, divine seizure and madness. For whenever the light of God shines upon us, human light is extinguished and when the divine sun sets, the human dawns and rises. This is what is apt to happen to the guild of the prophets. At the arrival of the divine spirit, our mind is evicted. When the spirit departs, the wandering mind returns home, for it is well established that that which is subject to death may not share a home with that which is deathless. Therefore the eclipse of the power of reason and the darkness that envelops it begets ecstasy and inspired madness.[48]

Compare the foregoing descriptions with Paul's account of his out-of-body ascent:

> I must go on boasting. Although there is nothing to be gained, I will go on to visions and revelations from the Lord. I know a man in Christ who fourteen years ago was caught up to the third heaven. Whether it was in the body or out of the body I do not know–God knows. And I know that this man–whether in the body or apart from the body I do not know, but God knows–was caught up to paradise and heard inexpressible things, things that no one is permitted to tell. (2 Cor. 12:1-4)

This observation is of special relevance to our study: "All cultures contain techniques that facilitate the controlled occurrence of [temporal lobe transients]; most have been selected and maintained on the basis of their consequences: mystical experiences."[49] Music, motion, and memory can be used to "kindle" or induce a microseizure in circuits associated with emotion, motivation and memory, broadly labeled the *limbic system*, so named because the region forms the *border* or *limbus* between the cortex and the deep structures of the brain stem; structures within the limbic system are "highly susceptible to seizure induction."[50]

Given that "a pleasant or ecstatic experience"–including sexual orgasm[51]–can result from some microseizures, and that they are relatively easy to induce, it comes as no surprise "that the subject learns how to use the adequate stimulus in order to get a self-induced seizure."[52] Eusapia Palladino, a trance medium investigated by the Society for Psychical Research, is a classic example of sexually ecstatic trance–she would "customarily wake from her séances hot, sweaty and aroused" and "she would sometimes shudder with pleasure as a phantom lover drew her to orgasm."[53] (A sense of euphoria is sometimes the initial stage of psychosis as well.)[54]

It would not be surprising if the prophets and visionaries who populate the Bible were subjects who had learned how to "kindle" their own mystical experiences and likely rather enjoyed them. A study of subjects who had near-death experiences (NDEs) found that 80% reported auditory hallucinations afterward and that "a large majority of those respondents with auditory hallucinations would rather keep hearing the voices than have them go away."[55] The findings of a number of surveys and studies suggest that symptoms often associated with insanity may in fact contain hidden rewards, a concept familiar to those with a background in healthcare generally.

Large surveys have repeatedly confirmed that ten to fifteen percent of "nonclinical" respondents report hallucinations "without presenting with other pathological symptoms" and that women are more likely than men to have such experiences.[56] Indeed some well-known theologies turn consensus reality on its head; in Hinduism the *atman*, or soul, can be caught in *maya*, the illusion of the material body and all things connected to it, and some indigenous peoples believe "that all normal human experience is a hallucination and ayahuasca provides access to veridical reality."[57]

Early Christianity shared this upside-down metaphysics. Origen, for example, claims that believers see beyond the material world, having "a superior and incorporeal sense,"[58] not unlike moderns who have supposedly "received special spiritual insights and communion with God, which consists of a heightened ability to perceive spiritual reality and heightened rationality."[59] Or as Paul has it, "these are the things God has revealed to us by his Spirit" (1 Cor. 2:10). Of course, Christians who claim supernatural insight into realities divine routinely deny similar claims of supernatural insight on the part of other religions.

Scrutiny of the writings of mystics such as Paul, Ignatius of Loyola, and Teresa of Avila leads some authorities to suggest "simple partial seizures" (SPS's) as a source of "epileptic consciousness" during which the subject "contemplates what happens in his mind as an astonished onlooker . . . the experience has a tone of extraordinary clarity, which can even form the illusion of wonderful illumination."[60] Given his references to his "surpassingly great revelations" (2 Cor. 12:7) and being caught up to paradise, to say nothing of seeing a light, falling to the ground while hearing a voice (Acts 22:6-7), and suffering from temporary blindness afterward, not a few have noted that Paul's "account bears a close resemblance to the psychic and perceptual experience of a temporal lobe seizure." Landsborough describes a number of seizures accompanied by temporary loss of vision.[61]

A correlation between heightened religiosity and epilepsy has been documented since the 19th century, encompassing a spectrum of interior experiences that include visual and auditory hallucinations and a seizure "which included a vision of 'Christ coming down from the sky.'"[62] Dewhurst discusses the circumstances of six modern cases of religious conversion following seizures, and observes of Paul's case specifically, "He fell down and suddenly experienced visual and auditory hallucinations with photism and transient blindness. As a direct result of this experience he was converted to Christianity."[63]

Contrary to typical seizure presentation, which has never been considered a mental illness in modern times, it is now widely recognized that "schizotypal personality" predisposes some subjects to "unusual perceptual experiences" including "shamanic-like journeying experiences."[64] The symptoms of *schizotypy*, which are similar to symptoms of psychosis but milder, are relatively common: Ten to fifteen percent of the general population has experienced "some kind of hallucinatory experience" and twenty percent "report delusions ... psychotic-like phenomenology is 50 times more prevalent than the narrower, medical concept of schizophrenia."[65]

Studies of schizotypy or "psychosis-proneness" have established that there is no "fool-proof distinction" between spiritual experiences and psychosis and one found that upon testing, "a group of chronically deluded individuals had comparable scores to a sample of Anglican Ordinands ... who were as persuaded of the veracity of their experiences as the deluded in-patients." The *clinically* deluded were "all in-patients at the Maudsley and Bethlem hospitals,"[66] London psychiatric facilities. A more benign explanation for "psychic experiences is also possible—an estimated "70% to 80% of the people reporting psychic experiences appear to be misinterpreting the experience."[67]

A number of psychological studies have also addressed cognitive differences between believers and nonbelievers. In general those prone to fantasy are more apt to have paranormal experiences as well as intense religious experiences. It is clear from psychological studies that the tendency to believe in ghosts or other paranormal phenomena exists across a spectrum that ends in pathology, "a pattern of reality testing deficits" that lends itself to "the formation of psychotic beliefs," as well as "poor probability reasoning."[68]

We are all familiar with *pareidolia*, the tendency to see a meaningful religious image in a random pattern, an image of Jesus perceived on toasted bread, or the Virgin Mary in a cloud formation. Similarly, a poor grasp of probability leads "prayer warriors" to count the hits and ignore the misses. Seeing hidden meaning in unassociated events explains the frequent link the psychiatrically religious make between natural disasters and terrorist attacks and feminism and gay pride parades to cite a persistently recurring pattern from the United States.

"Delusions arise in part because inferences are not subjected to a rigorous process of reality testing... nor are they given similar reassessment as further relevant information comes to hand."[69] *Cognitive closure* is an additional tendency characteristic of paranormal belief systems. Also known as "seize and freeze," cognitive closure refers to the habitual inclination to form a rigid opinion that is not subject to later disconfirmation by contrary evidence.

A related propensity is *confirmation bias*, the acceptance of evidence that corroborates belief but the rejection of evidence that contradicts it.[70] Like baked-in religious confidence, a "key characteristic of a psychotic delusion is that it carries a very high level of conviction . . . a delusion therefore tends to be impervious to counterargument."[71] A potentially complete list of cognitive biases that underlie beliefs for which there is weak evidence at best is beyond the focus of this book; fortunately such a list is readily available.[72]

We have no reason to think that Paul's ecstatic experiences were anything less than completely real *to him*. That said, apologist true believers who insist that Paul's religious experiences should also be real *to us* must first explain why his reports, which exactly match the extensively documented symptoms of temporal lobe seizures, are better explained as communications from Jesus repeatedly appearing and speaking from beyond the grave.

Like psychologist Isabel Clarke, I really do wonder how "psychosis and spirituality have been kept so distinct." Clarke says it "demands explanation." I agree, and also suspect that preservation "of the prevailing orthodoxy in which much has been invested" is the best explanation for the distinction.[73] After all, we have no problem suspecting new religious movements like the Branch Davidians of being examples of *folie à plusieurs,* cases of mass insanity, while calmly accepting the equally improbable claims of older religious traditions.

It would come as no surprise that people who are already "churched up" would tend to explain their feelings of elation or sudden insight within a religious framework. Religious thinking is notoriously open-ended in that regard, "well adapted for explaining apparently incongruous information . . . practically any event can be interpreted as an example of 'God working in mysterious ways.'"[74] Interpreting the resurrection as a physical body leaving the tomb presents the reader with impossibilities. It should come as no surprise that some have at least suggested psychological explanations; to many, if not most "modern Christians . . . the true significance of the Resurrection was inner and spiritual rather than external and physical . . . the Resurrection has become a problem of psychology rather than history."[75]

1 Corinthians 15

According to Paul, arguably Christianity's foremost spokesman, belief in the resurrection is both the cornerstone of Christian belief and the basis of Christian hope:

> But if it is preached that Christ has been raised from the dead, how can some of you say that there is no resurrection from the dead? If there is no resurrection from the dead, then not even Christ has been raised. And if Christ has not been raised, our preaching is useless and so is your faith. More than that, we are then found to be false witnesses about God, for we have testified about God that he raised Christ from the dead. For if the dead are not raised, then Christ has not been raised either. And if Christ has not been raised, your faith is futile; you are still in your sins. Then those also who have fallen asleep in Christ are lost. If only for this life we have hope in Christ, we are of all people most to be pitied. (1 Cor. 15:12-19)

Clearly, some within Paul's churches doubted the veracity of the resurrection, at least as Paul preached it. Otherwise there would be no point to Paul's question, "How can some of you say that there is no resurrection from the dead?" Who these Christians were who denied the resurrection and why they denied it "is a very complex and highly disputed issue"[76] in New Testament scholarship as the voluminous literature on the topic attests.

Since Paul does not identify them or their reasons, there is no firm basis for establishing their identity. No one really knows who the deniers were or what, specifically, they denied, or even if Paul misunderstood the deniers or misrepresented their belief.[77] In any event, two generations after Paul's letter to the Corinthians we are informed that some Christians claimed, "the resurrection has already taken place" (2 Tim. 2:18).

For Paul, Jesus' miracles—which he never even mentions—are not the decisive factor for belief. Even though half the books of the New Testament have been attributed to Paul, he rarely refers to Jesus' teachings, never quotes Jesus' parables. Nor does Paul ever allude to the virgin birth, the transfiguration, or the resurrection of figures such as Lazarus. In fact, Paul makes clear that he did not rely on the original community of believers for his information:

> I want you to know, brothers and sisters, that the gospel I preached is not of human origin. I did not receive it from any man, nor was I taught it; rather, I received it by revelation from Jesus Christ ... then after three years [in Arabia] I went up to Jerusalem to get acquainted with Cephas and stayed with him fifteen days. I saw none of the other apostles—only James, the Lord's brother. (Gal. 1:11-12, 18-19)

According to his own testimony, Paul knew only Peter (Cephas) among the apostles and met only a single relative of Jesus, his brother James. According to his own writings, Paul's idiosyncratic theology appears to have been derived "by revelation," visionary transports to "paradise" and "the third heaven" (2 Cor. 12:2-4).

It bears reiterating that Paul's gospel "is not of human origin" nor received from "any man" nor was he "taught it." Rather it was "*received by revelation* from Jesus Christ." As Maccoby observes, it is therefore not really accurate to speak of Paul's experience on the road to Damascus as a "conversion" since it presupposes

> that Christianity already existed before Paul had this experience, and that therefore all that was required was that Paul should be 'converted' to this already existing religion ... In fact, Christianity, as a religion separate from Judaism, stems from this event. Paul's vision of Jesus was the epiphany or divine appearance which initiated Christianity, just as the appearance of God in the burning bush initiated Judaism.[78]

We've seen already at the beginning of this chapter that Paul sought to validate his apostolic authority and support his idiosyncratic theology. Read critically, Paul's own letters suggest a strong self-aggrandizing motive for his "surpassingly great revelations" (2 Cor. 12:7) as well as his humble bragging.

Robinson notes that "the original disciples and Jesus' family, those who knew him when he was on earth, do not in any way outrank Paul, who never laid eyes on nor was even known to this Jesus."[79] He managed to become Protestant Christianity's foremost Apostle. But during his life, things didn't look quite so good for him. Paul's letters provide abundant evidence that his gospel and his authority were seriously contested then, leading James Harrison to remark, "It is an irony of history that by late antiquity Paul had become the authority figure he never was during his lifetime."[80]

Given Paul's incessant self-promotion, it would seem that "visions and revelations" were the primitive apostolic equivalent of today's credentialism—"I boast rather freely... we will not boast more than is befitting... Let the man who boasts boast in the Lord... nobody will stop my boasting... I may boast a little... I too will boast... If I must boast... I must go on boasting... I will boast about a man like that [*me, me!*]... I will boast even more gladly..." (2 Cor. 10-12).

That Paul was a visionary of sorts could hardly be denied—he sees Ananias "in a vision" (Acts 9:12), has another vision of a "man of Macedonia" (Acts 16:9), and another on the road to Damascus (Acts 22:6-7). While in Jerusalem, he reports, "I fell into a trance and saw the Lord speaking to me" (Acts 22:17-18). Regarding Paul, the Pharisees in the Sanhedrin ask, "What if a spirit or an angel has spoken to him?" (Acts 23:9) and "the following night the Lord stood near Paul" and spoke to him (Acts 23:11). During a storm at sea, "an angel of the God to whom I belong and whom I serve stood beside me and said, 'Do not be afraid, Paul'" (Acts 27:23-24). And these are only the visionary experiences reported in Acts!

Besides his reported visionary conversations, Paul evidently spent time conversing with spirits on many other occasions: "I thank God that I speak in tongues more than all of you" (1 Cor. 14:28). The letter to the Corinthians clearly establishes that "the services in Corinth were largely devoted to calling spirits and to expression of utterances the spirits were thought to inspire."[81] Paul refers to the Corinthians' enthusiasm at 1 Corinthians 4:12: "because *you are devotees of spirits* . . ."[82] Nearly all versions of the New Testament *interpret* rather than translate this passage by rendering it "gifts of the spirit" although spirit is clearly *plural* in the text and word for *gift*, *dōron*, occurs *nowhere* in the verse. That *multiple* spirits are being referred to is evident since "Paul himself, at the beginning of 1 Corinthians 12, gave a rule of thumb by which spirits could be judged: "If anyone speaking 'with a spirit' says 'Jesus is anathema,' that spirit is not 'of God.'"[83]

Indeed, it's clear that early Christians summoned multiple spirits: "do not believe every spirit, but test the spirits" (1 John 4:1), or "some will abandon the faith and follow deceiving spirits" (1 Tim. 4:1). "The form of early Christianity associated with Paul can be characterized as a spirit-possession cult. Paul establishes communities of those possessed by the spirit of Jesus."[84] "The worshippers and the attending spirits form a double assembly."[85]

Based on the evidence of his letters, it could be argued that Paul is simply following the globally attested pattern that Larøi describes:

> "the shaman-to-be usually must report certain kinds of phenomena that are understood by his or her broader social world to be the appropriate signs of the spirit . . . adding personal vivid detail demonstrates that the experience is authentic and not repeated as a cultural script. This pattern is common in these ethnographic and historical accounts of hallucinations."[86]

It is clear that early Christian communities were troubled by the question of the authenticity of visions, although in their culture the question was not framed as "real versus imaginary" but as "good versus evil spirits"–"do not believe every spirit, but test the spirits *to see whether they are from God*, for many false prophets have gone out into the world" (1 John 4:1). In modern studies of schizophrenics who hear voices, it has been established that those not deeply influenced by Western cultural norms were more likely "to describe conversational relationships with their voices" and to report "that their dominant external voice was God, and that hearing God was a good experience."[87]

It is fair to ask (as many have) what, if anything, did Paul really know about Jesus' death and burial? Or, for that matter, by the time the gospels were composed what did anyone really know about it? Like other New Testament stories, the accounts of Jesus' trial and execution are problematic. Although the fourth gospel claims Jesus' disciples removed his body and buried it (John 19:38), in Acts Paul is quoted as saying that "*those living in Jerusalem and their rulers* . . . asked Pilate to put [Jesus] to death, even as they fulfilled all the things written about him, and taking him down from the gibbet, *they* laid him in a tomb" (Acts 13:27-29).

As the text stands, exactly who "they" were that disposed of Jesus' body is unclear. Dale Allison draws attention to the ambiguous text of Acts, concluding that the record is consistent with Jesus' burial by Joseph of Arimathea:[88] "Burial by enemies, perhaps in a place for criminals (cf. m. Sanh. 6:5: t. Sanh. 9:8),[89] does not contradict Mark's basic content, which is that a member of the Sanhedrin interred Jesus. Observe also that the plurals of Acts 13:29 ("*they* took him down [*kathelontes*] . . . and [*they*] laid him in a tomb") match the plural of Mark 16:6: "the place where *they* laid [*ethēkan*] him. Mark too seems to imply that Joseph did not act alone (cf. also John 19:31, 39-42)."[90]

However, the probability that a member of the Sanhedrin, the body that condemned Jesus for blasphemy and then delivered him up to the Roman authority for crucifixion, would personally see to his burial has been vigorously denied. Lowder points out that

Rome "typically denied burial to victims of crucifixion" as well as that "Rabbinic law specifies that criminals may not be buried in tombs."[91] More to the point, the Joseph of Arimathea story is riddled with improbability.

According to the earliest gospel, the Sanhedrin's verdict was unanimous: "They *all* condemned him as worthy of death" (Mark 14:64), "the *whole* Sanhedrin" (Mark 15:1) delivered Jesus up to Pilate. Luke contradicts Mark on this point by claiming that Joseph was an exception (Luke 23:50). John even claims that Joseph and Nicodemus *personally* embalmed Jesus' body with spices and wrapped it in linen (John 19:39-42). If they had been about to celebrate the Passover with its attendant ritual, such physical contact with a corpse would have rendered them ceremonially unclean for seven days and unable to participate–"But some of them could not celebrate the Passover on that day because they were ceremonially unclean on account of a dead body" (Num. 9:6).

Paul, in his previous incarnation as Saul, was once an avid persecutor of the early church (Acts 7:5-8:1, 22:4-5) and may have known for a fact that the same authorities that executed Jesus were the ones who removed the body from the cross and disposed of it. It's been suggested that Paul may have had some relationship with the Temple police in a role of "enforcing Jewish religious law . . . in a punitive fashion, initiating policy, enforcing it with considerable zeal, and casting judgment against those caught,"[92] but there are also problems with this reconstruction of events.

According to the author of Acts, Saul "went to the high priest and asked him for letters to the synagogues in Damascus, so that if he found any there who belonged to the Way, whether men or women, he might take them as prisoners to Jerusalem" (Acts 9:2). However, the high priest, who functioned as the chief of police over the Temple and Judea, an authority given him by the Roman occupiers, *had no direct jurisdiction over synagogues*, much less in Damascus, a part of the Nabataean kingdom which was not under Roman rule.[93]

III: AN ABUNDANCE OF VISIONS

The passage usually cited as the earliest report of Jesus' post-resurrection appearances comes from a letter written by Paul:

> For I passed on to you as of first importance what I also received, that Christ died for our sins according to the scriptures, and that he was buried, and that he was raised on the third day according to the scriptures, and that he appeared to Cephas, then to the twelve, then he appeared to more than five hundred brothers at one time, the greater number of whom remain until now but some have fallen asleep.
>
> Then he appeared to James, then to all the apostles. Last of all, he appeared even to me, as to one born before his time. (1 Cor. 15:3-8)

The claim that Jesus appeared to five hundred witnesses at one time is the sort of exaggeration one would expect from a later apocryphal account, and the fact that none of the gospels, written decades after 1 Corinthians, report this amazing confirmation of the resurrection may mark the passage as an interpolation, a forgery inserted into the text after Paul's death. In any case, "a simple comparison of the Gospels and 1 Corinthians 15 shows that the two traditions cannot be reconciled."[94] Even apologetic writers must admit, "Paul's list of appearances in 1 Corinthians and the resurrection narratives in the gospels are remarkably–and puzzlingly–ill-matched."[95] The women at the tomb, the first witnesses of the empty tomb, are unmentioned as is Jesus' appearance on the road to Emmaus, nor do the gospels record an appearance to "James, the Lord's brother" (Gal. 1:19), presumably the James of 1 Corinthians 15.

If the passage is assumed to be genuine, "the very fact that Paul placed a lengthy list of the eyewitnesses of the appearances of the risen Jesus at the very beginning of the whole discussion [of the resurrection of believers] is most easily explained by the suggestion that the apostle feared some of his addressees entertained doubts on this matter."[96]

The core–"that Christ died... that he was buried... that he was raised... that he appeared"–is widely accepted to be "a four-line formula,"[97] an ancient confession of faith "handed down" and "received" in the early church. *Handed down* and *received* "are technical terms used by Jewish rabbis for the transmission of sacred tradition" and the "transliterated Aramaic [*Kēpha*] ("Cephas") for Peter"[98] can be taken as evidence for an ancient formulation and "the binding of the tradition to Cephas... connects the idea of the church firmly with Jerusalem."[99] As usual, however, there are problems with both the origin and interpretation of the passage, including "tensions" between the section and its context. The "language is not Paul's."[100]

The terms employed, particularly "at one time (*ephapax*)," have been taken by some to mean "that 1 Cor. xv 5-7 contains only a single appearance... all other occurrences of [*ephapax*] in the New Testament have this eschatological meaning,"[101] as in "the death [Jesus] died, he died... *once for all* (*ephapax*)" (Rom. 6:10). If construed to mean that 500 witnesses saw Jesus *simultaneously*, the passage would refer to an epiphany *en masse*, not an uncommon event in the past or present.[102]

Murphy-O'Connor tries to account for the adverb by noting that if Paul had simply written "he appeared to five hundred brothers," the "most natural interpretation would have been to understand it as a reference to a mass vision." Then the insertion of *ephapax* underscores "the objectivity of the experience."[103] Using apparitions of the Virgin Mary as an example, with thousands claiming the same vision, Snape remarked, "ecstasy and enthusiasm creates an epidemic of appearances." Living in "an atmosphere of apocalyptic... and believing that the Messiah was shortly coming," early Christians experienced a "psychical epidemic after hearing from the Galileans how Jesus had appeared to them."[104]

If derived from a doxology used in the early church, similar to "He appeared to angels, he was preached among the Gentiles" (1 Tim. 3:16), the appearances of Jesus in 1 Corinthians 15 have no more necessary connection to history than the lyrics of a Christmas carol. But if all or part is assumed to be original to Paul, then his admission, "some have fallen asleep," is addressed to "a community moving toward an expectation of fulfillment, but already marked by death."[105]

Likely no part of the New Testament has been the subject of more scholarly debate and commentary than 1 Corinthians 15. Even a brief summation of the controversies over its interpretations is far beyond the scope of this book, but the mere fact that such a short passage has provoked scores of conflicting opinions on both its authenticity as well as its meaning implies that no one to date has made a completely convincing case on either question.

If, as Paul claimed, his gospel was not received from men but rather revealed by God, would he even have bothered to quote a confession of faith that originated in the Jerusalem mother church with which he had bitterly quarreled? Whether the doxology originated in Jerusalem or elsewhere, "the binding of the tradition to Cephas and the twelve connects the idea of the church firmly with Jerusalem."[106] The extensive debate over what, if any, part of the five hundred witnesses story can be traced back to Paul also raises the possibility that *none* of it was written or quoted by Paul, but was inserted into a genuine letter at a later date. In other words, it may well be an interpolation that was intended to support belief in the resurrection.

That possibility is worth briefly considering, particularly given Paul's evident lack of concern for the "historical" Jesus:

> Paul lifts the [crucifixion] completely out of its contemporary context and treats it as a supernatural happening... at a very early stage in the life of the Church there already existed a significant diversity in the

evaluation of the historicity of that most fundamental of all events, namely, the Crucifixion.[107]

Paul transforms the significance of the Eucharist in similar fashion–"the Eucharist, as set forth by Paul, in effect lifts the historical event of the death of Jesus completely out of its setting in time and space and confers upon it that transcendental significance that characterizes . . . the various mystery-cults."[108]

First Corinthians is believed to have been composed around 55 CE. The earliest extensive manuscript that contains the letter, known to papyrologists as *P*46, has been tentatively dated from 175-225 CE. Over a century–perhaps nearly two centuries–may separate our earliest copy from the original. We have no originals of any ancient author including the authors of the books of the New Testament.

Without drowning in the details of how these ancient documents were copied, edited, and possibly corrupted, suffice to say that *no* current mainstream experts on the New Testament text claim we have *exactly* what the authors wrote. A leading textual critic has called our surviving documents the "interpretive text-form . . . as it was used in the life, worship, and teaching of the church," a text subject to "reformulations motivated by theological, liturgical, ideological, historical, stylistic, or other factors."[109]

Instances of *interpolated text*, which could represent a forged passage deliberately inserted into a text or a marginal note inserted by accident due to careless copying, are suspected in several of Paul's undisputed letters, including his earliest, 1 Thessalonians.[110] Suspect passages, thought to have been inserted into Paul's letters at some time after their composition, are generally tagged due to differences in style or to conflicts with "Pauline thought in general."[111] As many as seven interpolations have been proposed for 1 Corinthians alone.[112] Interpolations can rarely be ruled out by comparing the earliest manuscripts, given that "manuscript evidence for the Pauline letters goes back no further than the late

III: AN ABUNDANCE OF VISIONS

second century at best, and most of the evidence comes from the fourth century and later."[113]

Several motives can be advanced for creating forgeries attributed to Paul. Once his writings became authoritative for Christianity generally, the claim that Paul had written an epistle obviously became attractive. In mainstream New Testament studies, Colossians and Ephesians are widely recognized as probable forgeries, as is 2 Thessalonians, which ironically warns of "teaching allegedly from us—whether by a prophecy or by word of mouth or by letter" (2 Thess. 2:2). The "Pastoral Epistles," 1 and 2 Timothy and Titus, are unquestionably forgeries. It would therefore come as no surprise to find an early copyist's favorite bits of liturgy slipped into Paul's genuine writings, something Paul *could* have said or *would* have said had he only known about it.

A general suspicion of new religious ideas is a second powerful motive for fake attribution. Although most Greco-Roman intellectuals thought Judaism utterly bizarre, allowances were made for it given its undeniable antiquity. Assuming such a conservative mind-set, religious novelty could anticipate a cold reception, hence the impulse to falsely attribute recent works.

Robert Price has produced what is likely the most complete summation of the evidence that 1 Corinthians 15:3-11 is an interpolation. He lists the internal evidence that could indicate tampering with "a possible earlier state of the text," namely "aporias," or internal contradictions, "stylistic irregularities, anachronisms, and redactional seams,"[114] glitches in the text where its continuity appears disrupted. Price musters several lines of evidence, some already mentioned, such as Paul's lack of dependence on sources other than personal revelations, the lack of this astounding confirmation in the gospels, as well as the speculative and unconvincing attempts to harmonize the passage with other accounts of gathered disciples such as Pentecost.[115]

In any case, the verdict of the historian Robert Grant appears secure: "No word in this account [1 Corinthians 15:3-8] suggests that the appearances of Jesus were other than 'spiritual'; it was not the 'flesh and blood' of Jesus which the witnesses saw... what [Paul] saw, and what he believes other Christians saw, was the 'spiritual body' of Jesus."[116] Even apologetic writers who argue that Paul believed in the resurrection of some sort of transformed, spiritualized body concede that Paul never speaks of an empty tomb–"The word 'tomb' is not to be found in his Epistles."[117]

Notes

1. Genesis 49:29, Numbers 27:13, 31:2, Judges 2:10, for example.
2. Josephus, *Jewish War* IV, 324.
3. Rice & Stambough, op. cit., 169.
4. Seaford, *Dionysos*, 125.
5. Strelan, *Strange Acts*, 180.
6. Maccoby, op. cit., 107.
7. Brandon, *Numen* 2 (1955) 160, 162.
8. Walker, *Journal of Biblical Literature* 88 (1969) 162.
9. Murphy-O'Connor, *Catholic Biblical Quarterly* 43 (1981) 589.
10. Snape, op. cit., 195.
11. Lindars, *Bulletin of the John Rylands Library* 67 (1984-1985) 771.
12. Walker, *Journal of Biblical Literature* 88 (1969) 165.
13. Peters, et al., *British Journal of Clinical Psychology* 38 (1999) 93.
14. Wypustek, *Vigiliae Christianae* 51 (1997) 277.
15. Jackson, *Psychosis and Spirituality*, 168.
16. Lindeman & Svedholm, *Review of General Psychology* 16 (2012) 3.
17. Ibid, 7.
18. Menezes & Moreira-Almeida, *Current Psychiatry Reports* 12 (2010), n176: "The personality constructs of thin boundaries and transliminality are both reported to be associated with susceptibility to mental illness"; Kennedy, *Journal of Parapsychology* 69 (2005) 269.

    "Thin boundaries" and "transliminality" reflects "a tendency for unconscious processes to emerge into consciousness" (Kennedy, 267).
19. Trimble & Freeman, *Epilepsy and Behavior* 9 (2006) 408.
20. Lecouteux, op. cit., 125-28.
21. Erlendur, *Omega* 19 (1988-1989) 104.

22. Ibid, 107, 109.

23. Ibid, 111.

24. Vincent, *Journal of Near-Death Studies* 30 (2012) 142.

25. Ibid, 138, 142.

26. Ibid, 139.

27. Rose, op. cit., 275.

28. Craffert, *Religion and Theology* 15 (2008) 138-39.

29. Vaitl, et alia, *Psychological Bulletin* 131 (2005) 99.

30. Persinger, *Perceptual and Motor Skills* 57 (1983) 1257.

31. Compare Acts 2:2: "Suddenly a sound like the blowing of a violent wind came from heaven . . ."

32. Persinger, op. cit., 1257-58.

33. Ibid, 1257-59.

34. Frankfurter, *Harvard Theological Review* 103 (2010) 38.

35. Smith, *Transactions and Proceedings of the American Philological Association* 96 (1965) 407.

36. Montanari, op. cit., 1721.

37. Vaitl, op. cit., 107.

38. Rock, et al., *North American Journal of Psychology* 10 (2008) 79.

39. Walsh, *The Journal of Transpersonal Psychology* 21 (1989) 4.

40. Greyson & Liester, *Journal of Humanistic Psychology* 44 (2004) 321.

41. Kennedy, *Journal of Parapsychology* 69 (2005) 268.

42. *Transliminality*, "a hypothesized tendency for psychological material to cross thresholds into or out of consciousness," is the proposed "single dimension underlying variables such as magical ideation, mystical experience, dream interpretation and proneness to fantasy. Thalbourne, Crawley & Houran, *Personality and Individual Differences* 35 (2003) 1965.

43. Thalbourne, *Archiv für Religionspsychologie* 3 (2009) 375-86.

44. Thalbourne, et al., *Personality and Individual Differences* 35 (2003) 1966.

45. See Parker's discussion in *Vetus Testamentum* 28 (1978) 271-85.

46. Vaitl, op. cit., 105.

47. Parker, *Vetus Testamentum* 28 (1978) 282.

48. Philo, *Quis rerum divinarum heres*.

49. Persinger, op. cit., 1260.
50. Bertram, *Epilepsia* 48 (2007) 68.
51. Vaitl, op. cit., 104.
52. Alvarez-Rodriguez, *Health* 6 (2014) 2093.
53. Clarke, op. cit., 203.
54. Clarke, *Psychosis and Spirituality*, 137.
55. Greyson & Liester, op. cit., 328.
56. Menezes & Moreira-Almeida, *Current Psychiatry Reports* 12 (2010) 176.
57. Larøi, et al., *Schizophrenia Bulletin* 40 (2014) S214.
58. Origen, *Contra Celsum* I, 48.
59. Hauck, *Harvard Theological Review* 81 (1988) 246.
60. Alvarez-Rodriguez, op. cit., 2091.
61. Landsborough, *Journal of Neurology, Neurosurgery, and Psychiatry* 50 (1987) 659, 662-663.
62. Dewhurst & Beard, *British Journal of Psychiatry* 117 (1970) 497.
63. Ibid, 502.
64. Rock, et al., op. cit., 79.
65. Peters, *Psychosis and Spirituality*, 191, 193
66. Peters, et al., *British Journal of Clinical Psychology* 38 (1999) 83, 85, 88, 91.
67. Kennedy, op. cit., 264.
68. Dein, *International Journal of Transpersonal Studies* 31 (2012) 66-68.
69. Irwin, et al., *Australian Journal of Parapsychology* 12 (2012) 108.
70. Ibid, 108-109.
71. Ibid, 117.
72. Eller, *Christianity in the Light of Science*, 47-68.
73. Clarke, op. cit., 1.
74. Spilka, et al., *Journal for the Scientific Study of Religion* 24 (1985) 13.
75. Cheek, *Journal of Bible and Religion* 27 (1959) 191.
76. Sider, *Novum Testamentum* 19 (1977) 125. The complexities of who the deniers were and why they denied the resurrection is explored at length by Horsley, *Novum Testamentum* 20 (1978) 203-31.
77. Wedderburn, *Novum Testamentum* 23 (1981) 229-41.
78. Maccoby, *The Mythmaker*, 103-104.

79. Robinson, *Journal of Biblical Literature* 101 (1982) 21.

80. Harrison, *Vigiliae Christianae* 58 (2004) 24.

81. Morton Smith, *Harvard Theological Review* 73 (1980) 244.

82. My translation of *epei zēlōtai este pneumatōn*.

83. Smith, op. cit., 245.

84. Mount, *Journal of Biblical Literature* 124 (2005) 316.

85. Thee, *Julius Africanus and the Early Christian View of Magic*, 382.

86. Larøi, op. cit., S215.

87. Ibid, S217.

88. Joseph of Arimathea, who supposedly asked Pilate for permission to bury Jesus in his own tomb (Matt. 27:58).

89. The *Mishnah Sanhedrin* and *Tractate Sanhedrin*, sections of the Talmud that deal with criminal jurisprudence.

90. Allison, *Resurrecting Jesus*, 357.

91. Lowder, *Journal of Higher Criticism* 8 (2001) 254-55.

92. Reimer, *Miracle and Magic*, 65-66.

    "[F]rom the time of Coponius, the first *praefectus* of Judea (around 6 CE), all the power was concentrated in the hands of the Roman ruler; the Jewish authorities were reduced to a council around the high priest, whose authority concerned only Temple matters. Even the priestly garments and ornaments for the festivals were controlled by the Romans," Nodet, *Biblica* 91 (2010), 368.

93. Maccoby, *The Mythmaker*, 85-88.

94. Riley, *Resurrection Reconsidered*, 89. That the traditions appear incompatible doesn't mean harmonizing them hasn't been attempted repeatedly. See Gilmour, "The Christophany to More Than Five Hundred Brethren," *Journal of Biblical Literature* 80 (1961) 248-52, for example.

95. Bauckham, *The Laing Lecture at London Bible College*, 2.

96. Sider, *Novum Testamentum* 19 (1977) 132.

97. Pickup, *Journal of the Evangelical Theological Society* 56 (2013) 511.

98. Macgregor, *Journal of the Evangelical Theological Society* 49 (2006) 226.

99. Conzelmann, *Interpretation* 20 (1966) 22.

100. Ibid, 18.

101. Kearney, *Novum Testamentum* 22 (1980) 265-66.

102. Herman, op. cit., 151-52.

103. Murphy-O'Connor, op. cit., 586.
104. Snape, op. cit., 196-97.
105. Kearney, op. cit., 282.
106. Conzelmann, op. cit., 22.
107. Brandon, *Numen* 2 (1955) 159.
108. Ibid, 167.
109. Epp, *Harvard Theological Review* 92 (1999) 277.
110. Pearson, *Harvard Theological Review* 64 (1971) 79-94.
111. Schmidt, *Journal of Biblical Literature* 102 (1983) 276.
112. Murphy-O'Connor, *Catholic Biblical Quarterly* 48 (1986) 81-94.
113. Walker, *Catholic Biblical Quarterly* 50 (1988) 629-30.
114. Price, *Journal of Higher Criticism* 2 (1995) 71.
115. Ibid, 69-99.
116. Grant, *Journal of Religion* 28 (1948) 125.
117. Mánek, *Novum Testamentum* 2 (1958) 277.

IV

The Resurrection As Ghost Story

> No religion is based primarily on theology. First comes the story; and later, when the imaginative fires have died down and the myth-making faculty has ceased, along come the theologians to try to turn the story into a system.
>
> —Hyam Maccoby, *The Mythmaker*.

The Empty Tomb

We first hear of the empty tomb in the gospel of Mark. (Paul, who writes the first defense of the resurrection belief, never mentions one.) The women who discover the tomb to be empty encounter a nameless "young man" there who tells them that Jesus "is going ahead of you into Galilee. There you will see him, just as he told you" (Mark 16:7). At this point, the women flee in terror and tell no one about what they have seen.

This story, as transmitted in the manuscripts judged most likely to have preserved authentic text, seems remarkable deficient, unlikely to inspire confidence in the resurrection, and the ending of Mark has accordingly been the source of endless debate and speculation. As Peter Kirby remarks, "The ability of Mark to end this way, for whatever reason he had, suggests that the story did not exist before the writing of Mark."[1] That *the empty tomb proved Jesus' resurrection* has always been an implausible claim given how many *more likely* explanations could be advanced—Jesus' body had been moved, or the women were mistaken, or Jesus had never been placed in the tomb to begin with.

Using Mark as a primary source, Matthew and Luke set about repairing Mark's theological shortcomings; their editing supports Kirby's conclusion that had the story "been known far and wide, from the beginning of Christianity... the author of Mark would not have received it in this form."[2] As Lincoln observes, Matthew's revision—"So [the women] departed quickly from the tomb with fear and great joy, and ran to tell his disciples" (Matt. 28:8)–"is the ending the reader expects, and that is the ending one of the story's first-century readers, Matthew, has in fact supplied."[3]

Michael Goulder characterizes the ending of Mark as "such a tissue of contradictions as to defy credulity"[4] and it is widely recognized that the Passion narrative in Mark "raises a grave historical difficulty"[5] in terms of its chronology, specifically conflicting accounts in the gospels about the timing of Jesus' arrest and crucifixion. Mark creates "a calendar discrepancy, since according to John the Friday of Jesus' crucifixion fell on the *eve* of Passover (Nisan 14), but for the Synoptics it fell on the *day* of Passover (Nisan 15)."[6]

If Jesus was arrested, tried and crucified *before* Passover began–the trial "was the day of *Preparation of the Passover*; it was about noon" (John 19:14)–then it was clearly impossible for him to eat Passover with his disciples as claimed by Mark:

> On the first day of the Festival of Unleavened Bread, the day the lambs for the Passover meal were killed, Jesus' disciples asked him, "Where do you want us to go and get the Passover meal ready for you?" ... The disciples left, went to the city, and found everything just as Jesus had told them; and *they prepared the Passover meal*. (Mark 14:12, 16)

"It is plain, therefore, that two conflicting traditions were current in the apostolic church concerning the date of the crucifixion in relation to the Passover."[7] John has the legs of the two men crucified with Jesus broken to hasten their death (John 19:31). But according to John, Jesus has already died and his legs are not broken, a circumstance that identifies Jesus with the Passover lamb–"Do not break any of the bones" (Exodus 12:46). Kennard characterized this edit as "a clumsy attempt to present [Jesus] as an anti-type of the Paschal lamb."[8] Burkill observes, "the last supper could not have been the celebration of the Christian paschal feast" and concludes that John's gospel contains no account of the "institution of the Eucharist" to avoid the contradiction between his gospel and the Synoptics.[9]

By the time of the New Testament, the Lord's Supper has been merged with the Passover and Jesus with the Passover lamb–"Christ, our Passover lamb, has been sacrificed" (1 Cor. 5:7). The gospel of John accordingly has Jesus die on the afternoon of "the day of Preparation" (John 19:31), the afternoon *before* Passover, which began at sundown. John is clear–crystal clear–that Jesus died *before* Passover.

The Jewish leaders avoid entering Pilate's *praetorium* so as not to be defiled *before* Passover: "it was *early morning*, and to avoid ceremonial uncleanness they did not enter the palace, *because they wanted to be able to eat the Passover*" (John 18:28). John moves Jesus' crucifixion back to the afternoon *before* the evening Passover meal, back to the time when the lambs are being ritually slaughtered, to make the death of Jesus coincide with the death of the lambs. Hence, "Behold the Lamb of God that takes away the sin of the world!" (John 1:29). Kodell notes that it is

> surprising to find that on a matter treated so reverently and carefully as the Last Supper, the pattern of a privileged ceremony among Christians, there are so many discrepancies among the accounts and so many uncertainties about exactly what happened at the Supper and what it meant.[10]

Really, it's astounding that, by "the time our narratives were gathered together, probably no one knew what the exact course of events or the precise wording of Jesus' statements at the Supper had been." Kodell seems to downplay that even while pointing it out, concluding that it was only important that the narratives "agreed in their reports."[11] Alas, we know they failed in that respect as well.

Arguably, an empty tomb was not at first a symbol of Jesus' victory over death, but a problem that required an explanation. During its first few centuries "many Christians, often the most educated and often in the majority," agreed with pagan opponents "that the claim that anyone might rise bodily from the dead" was patently absurd as well as disgusting.[12] The epistle of *Polycarp to the Philippians* (circa 125 CE) denounces those who say "there is neither a resurrection nor a judgment," an opinion apparently held by "*many*."[13]

The early church addressed the disaster of the rejected and crucified Messiah by claiming that the rejection of Jesus had been foretold[14] and by folding these *ex eventu* predictions into the resurrection narrative. The "causal sequence" involved in creating such epiphany stories is well understood: "reports are taken up and amplified by partisan believers" and the "reports may also be embroidered and expanded upon by writers... giving rise to literary fictions."[15]

Examination of the texts of the later gospels that use Mark as a source reveals just such amplification. A psychological adjustment to Jesus' arrest and crucifixion is also evidenced by the response in the final gospel, John, that the unforeseen tragedy had long been part of God's inscrutable plan–"You would have no power over me if it were not given to you from above" (19:11). Jesus' reversals and misadventures "fulfill the scriptures," are "foreseen by the prophets," and are the fault of the recalcitrant Jews, rather common examples of displacement and scapegoating.[16]

Clearly, Jesus' death by crucifixion came as an unwelcome shock. His disciples "had hoped that he was the one who was going to redeem Israel" (Luke 24:21). Their reaction followed a common religious script: reframe the tragedy as the unfolding of a design that had previously been unrecognized,[17]–"This man was handed over to you by God's deliberate plan and foreknowledge" (Acts 2:23). As Allison points out, "God raised Jesus from the dead"[18] "is already *interpretation* rather than a straightforward statement of experience" (emphasis added).[19]

It's also clear that "embroidered additions"[20] were added to the bare story of Mark. The "young man" at the tomb in Mark (Mark 16:5) becomes an angel in Matthew (28:2), two men in shining garments in Luke (24:4), and two angels in John (20:12). Matthew solves the problem of who will roll away the stone for the women (Mark 16:3) by adding an angel that conveniently descends from heaven (Matt. 28:2), and has the women go to the tomb not to anoint Jesus' body, but simply to look at the grave site (Matt. 28:1).

The gospel stories of the resurrection raised at least as many questions as they answered and, moreover, represented only one of several theological solutions as evidenced by Paul's accusation that some in his churches rejected the idea of the resurrection—"how can some of you say there is no resurrection of the dead?" (1 Cor. 15:12). In fact, as the New Testament itself points out, some early Christians did "not confess that Jesus Christ is come in the flesh" (2 John 7).

Indeed, some passages in the New Testament could have rather easily been interpreted as denying that Jesus "had a real human body": Jesus possessed the "form," "likeness," or "appearance" (Phil. 2:7-8) of a man, "which gave at least license, if not mandate, to anyone who wished to deny to Jesus human flesh on either side of the grave."[21] Whatever the case, as many have pointed out, "If we are to account for the birth of the church, we must, one way or another, get Jesus raised from the dead, at least in the minds of the disciples . . . Either God raised Jesus from the dead, or the disciples somehow got the job done in their imaginations."[22] Some element of creative writing was probably involved in confecting the resurrection accounts, given that "the later the gospel the greater the detail and the more precise the story becomes."[23]

After listing the typical sort of "edits" characteristic of Luke's use of Mark, Marshall concludes,

> There is scarcely a feature of [Luke's resurrection] story which cannot be accounted for in this way [editing of Mark], and the conclusion is that the story has been invented by Luke, no doubt on the brief mention of burial in 1 Corinthians 15:3-5 . . . the conclusion is unavoidable that Luke has created the whole story.[24]

Peter Kirby lists four historically plausible scenarios besides the traditional explanation for the empty tomb: Jesus "was left hanging on the cross for the birds," the Romans dumped the corpse in a mass grave, the Jewish authorities buried the body, or the disciples buried the body and it remained in a tomb.[25] That Jesus was even buried after his execution continues to be vigorously contested–by longstanding tradition criminals "had no right to a ritual burial."[26]

Controversy about the burial of Jesus specifically arises from his conviction of *maiestas*, or treason, as "King of the Jews" (Matt. 27:37). Those condemned of treason were typically "denied normal sepulture... refusing burial to offenders against the state."[27] Lowder comments that the claim that Joseph of Arimathea buried Jesus (John 19:38-42) is improbable "given Joseph's membership in the very council that condemned Jesus."[28]

Certain specific elements of the resurrection stories also seem improbable, in particular the report that two days elapsed before the women arrived to anoint the body–"it was impossible in the climate of Palestine for a body to remain for two and a half days in a condition fit for being anointed with unguents."[29] According to Mark, "Mary Magdalene, Mary the mother of James, and Salome bought spices so that they might go to anoint Jesus' body" (Mark 16:1). The gospel of John, on the other hand, specifies that Joseph of Arimathea and Nicodemus had *already* embalmed Jesus' body with spices and wrapped it in linen–"Taking Jesus' body, the two of them wrapped it, with the spices, in strips of linen. This was in accordance with Jewish burial customs" (John 19:39-41). Did the women really intend to unwrap the *now putrefying* body and anoint it with spices?

Miller points out several barriers that prevent us from "making concrete decisions about the historical value of specific passages." Among those is evidence that "is spotty, sparse, and amenable to multiple interpretations," "nearly non-existent" traditions on which the gospels might be based, "intractable disagreements about fundamental issues of historical method," and relationships among the sources of the gospels that "are all open to legitimate debate."[30] Worse yet, according to some skeptical opinion, the oral tradition on which the gospels are presumably based,

> originated, not with Jesus, but in the church . . . This oral tradition contained no words of Jesus and no events in his career before his death . . . the material passed down to us cannot possibly be direct reports from the disciples . . . the material alleged to be from oral tradition contains language and points of view that are improbable on the lips of Jesus. The content often indicates that the material originated with the problems and issues in the church.[31]

The issues around the historicity of the stories are not clarified by the addition of details—legends are often rich in *completely fabricated detail*—as the mutually incompatible infancy stories in Matthew and Luke demonstrate. The Roman writer Phlegon of Tralles evidently used questionable details "to anchor a story in reality by reporting the exact place and/or time the miraculous event took place."[32]

Several plausible explanations exist for why, after two days, the first visitors to the tomb would find it empty. The body might have been removed and buried elsewhere: "Since the grave seen by the women was only temporary, removal of the body to its permanent resting place explains what became of it."[33] It has also been argued that Mark, the earliest gospel account, ends with an empty tomb but no appearance of Jesus because a *translation*—the abrupt disappearance of one taken to heaven, not a *resurrection*—was the intended meaning. In that case "it would have been the body's absence, not its presence, that would have signaled the provocative moment for the ancient reader."[34] We'll further explore the translation option in connection with the translation story of Romulus.

Concerning the probable disposal of Jesus' body, Crossan describes "the hierarchy of horror" that entailed not only the loss of life and possessions, but even the "destruction of identity" that included the utter corruption of the flesh of the condemned, in some cases even the murder of his family, and "the final penalty," being unburied, with no tomb to memorialize him, no grave that might be visited. The worst penalties included being burned alive, thrown to the beasts, and crucifixion, which in the last case "the body was left on the cross until birds of prey had destroyed it." Crossan concludes, "I keep thinking of all those thousands of other Jews crucified around Jerusalem in that terrible first century from among whom we have found only one skeleton and one nail. I think I know what happened to their bodies, and I have no reason to think Jesus' body did not join them."[35]

The magical and necromantic use of "relics" obtained from those violently killed as crucified criminals is well attested. Thus Jesus' body, the crucifixion nails, and even the wood of the cross would have been tempting targets for theft.[36] "One can also envisage a sorcerer, keen on body parts for magical ritual, stealing Jesus' corpse."[37]

Once the Christian practice of collecting post-mortem remains to use as miraculous relics became known to the Romans, "some governors used soldiers to keep believers from taking bodies and then took the further step of rendering the bodily remains entirely inaccessible."[38] In any case, Matthew reports that the Jewish authorities suspected Jesus' disciples would come by night to steal his body and claim that Jesus had been raised. Matthew–the true identity of the author is unknown, but following convention we'll call him "Matthew"–who is thought to have written his gospel forty or fifty years after Jesus' death,[39] probably included this bit of narrative to counter charges that Jesus' disciples had stolen his body, charges likely in circulation when he composed his gospel:

> The next day, the one after Preparation Day, the chief priests and the Pharisees went to Pilate. "Sir," they said, "we remember that while he was still alive that deceiver said, 'After three days I will rise again.' So give the order for the tomb to be made secure until the third day. Otherwise, his disciples may come and steal the body and

tell the people that he has been raised from the dead. This last deception will be worse than the first."

"Take a guard," Pilate answered. "Go make the tomb as secure as you know how." So they went and made the tomb secure by putting a seal on the stone and posting a guard. (Matt. 27:62-66)

How Matthew, who wrote his gospel two generations after Jesus' death, knew the contents of a private conversation between the Jewish leaders and the Roman administrator is anybody's guess.

Apart from the text of 1 Corinthians 15:3-8, the gospel of Mark becomes the oldest report of the resurrection:

When the Sabbath had passed, Mary the Magdalene and Mary the mother of James and Salome bought spices so they might go and anoint him, and very early in the morning on the first day of the week, the sun having risen, they went to the tomb. They were saying to one another, "Who will roll the stone away from the door of the tomb for us?"

Looking up, they saw that the stone—which was very large—had been rolled away and as they entered the tomb they saw a young man clothed in a white robe, sitting off to the right, and they were alarmed. But he said to them, "Do not be alarmed. You are seeking Jesus of Nazareth who was crucified. He is not here. He has been raised. Look at the place where they laid him! But go tell his disciples and Peter that he goes ahead of you into Galilee. You will see him there just as he told you."

And after they left, they fled from the tomb, for trembling and panic seized them. And they said nothing to anyone because they were afraid. (Mark 16:1-8)

It's been proposed that the "young man clothed in a white robe, *sitting off to the right*" (Mark 16:5) is not merely some "superfluous detail," but was meant as "a christological symbol" based on other Markan references—"you will see the Son of Man sitting at the right hand of power and coming on the clouds of heaven" (Mark 14:62). Citing a number of scholars, Scroggs and Groff point out, "many early Christians understood the resurrection of Jesus not in terms of appearance on earth, but rather as exaltation to heaven and enthronement"[40] at the right hand of God.

Throughout the Mediterranean world, even the dead were expected to be up and around by early morning, a belief that persists even today in the form of Easter "sunrise services." The soul of the dead "finally departed at the coming of dawn."[41] That would have been familiar to the Egyptians, whose "Spell for Coming Forth By Day" has the deceased emerging from the tomb into the daylight even as the sun emerged from the Underworld at the coming of dawn.[42] Three days in the tomb may reflect the common belief that the soul remained in the vicinity of the tomb for three days following burial until bloating and overt signs of decay made the face unrecognizable even to its former inhabitant.[43]

The resurrection account in Mark contradicts our expectations for several reasons, primarily because there are *no direct witnesses* to Jesus' resurrection in Mark or any of the other canonical gospels. The gospel accounts are also inconsistent about who or what the women really saw. Once the women arrive at the tomb, they do not actually see Jesus, but a "young man" (Mark 16:5) according to Mark, an "angel" according to Matthew (28:5), or "two men" according to Luke (24:4). In short, there is "no physical demonstration of Jesus' post-mortem body"[44] at the empty tomb in Mark. Moreover, in the earliest gospel account there is no sense of reassurance—the women flee in panic, too frightened to speak of their experience, and tell no one (Mark 16:8).

Compounding these inconsistencies are the conflicting instructions Jesus gives the disciples about where he will appear to them, *back in Galilee on a mountain*—"tell his disciples: 'He has risen from the dead and is going ahead of you into Galilee. There you will see him.' Then the eleven disciples went to Galilee" (Matt. 28:10, 16)–*or in Jerusalem in a locked room*–"he gave them this command: 'Do not leave Jerusalem, but wait for the gift my Father promised . . .'" (Acts 1:4)**45**

Before moving on to the particulars of the post-resurrection accounts, we must first pose a simple question: Why would the empty tomb, for which so many natural explanations might be advanced, be interpreted as evidence of resurrection? Given the fervent expectation of an apocalypse that would end in the general resurrection–"I know he will rise again in the resurrection on the last day" (John 11:24), the discovery or even the rumor of an empty tomb might be understood as the beginning of the resurrection.**46**

The presupposition of an imminent judgment might also explain Matthew's bizarre story of the "saints" awakening at the moment of Jesus' death and emerging from their tombs after his resurrection (Matt. 27:52-53), and Paul's reference to Jesus as the "firstfruits" of the resurrection (1 Cor. 15:23), as well as the reference to Jesus as the "firstborn" of the dead (Col. 1:18). As the hope of an immediate Parousia dimmed, support for the idea of another life in the hereafter came to rely on seeing apparitions–of Jesus and others–appearing as if still alive.

Women as Witnesses

The first of several inconsistencies with the discovery of the empty tomb is the reaction of the women and the male disciples. According to Mark, Jesus foretells his death and resurrection on *three* occasions,**47** specifying, "*Three days later he will rise*" (Mark 10:34). "Yet nothing in the behavior of these women on the Easter morning suggests that they expected to find anything extraordinary."**48** The women bring spices (Mark 16:1), expect the tomb to be sealed by a stone (Mark 16:3), and are alarmed to find the tomb empty (Mark 16:5). Finding the tomb empty, the women are not moved to the belief that Jesus has been raised, but propose a *naturalistic* explanation: "They have taken my Lord away," she said, "and I don't know where they have put him" (John 20:13).

A further difficulty with Mark's account, from the point of view of ancient society, is the lack of male witnesses to the empty tomb. Women at the tomb became a major point of weakness in the resurrection narrative–Christian women "were expressly targeted as unreliable witnesses, possessed, fanatical, sexual libertines, domineering of or rebellious toward their husbands..."[49] The women as the first witnesses to the empty tomb "is early and firmly entrenched" in the gospel tradition as is "the embarrassment around that fact."[50]

Celsus, a pagan who was critical of the irrational, emotionally driven nature of Christian belief, wrote this skeptical retort to the resurrection accounts sometime late in the 2nd century:

> While [Jesus] was alive he did not help himself, but after death he rose again and showed the marks of his punishment and how his hands had been pierced. But who say this? A hysterical female, as you say, and perhaps some other one of those who were deluded by the same sorcery, who either dreamt in a certain state of mind and through wishful thinking had a hallucination due to some mistaken notion (an experience which has happened to thousands), or, which is more likely, wanted to impress the others by telling this fantastic tale, and so by this cock-and-bull story to provide a chance for other beggars.[51]

Robin Lane Fox notes the likelihood that "women were a clear majority" in the early church. Of the writings of pagan moralists, he observes, "It was a well-established theme... that strange teachings appealed to leisured women who had just enough culture to admire it and not enough education to exclude it."[52] "Ardent credulity was presented as a weakness characteristic of the [female] sex, pagan or Christian."[53] For whatever it's worth, modern surveys have shown that belief in the paranormal is characteristic of "socially marginal groups," including the poorly educated, the young, and women.[54] Women do appear to score "significantly higher than males" on measurements of traditional religious belief and magical thinking.[55]

Women featured prominently in the Gentile churches established by Paul, although likely much less so in the Jerusalem mother church. Romans 16:1 describes "our sister Phoebe" as a minister (*diakonos*) "of the church in Cenchreae." (The participial construction should probably be taken to mean "serving [continuously] as a minister.") Paul uses the term *diakonos*, from whence *deacon*, of himself,[56] and mentions Andronicus and Junia, a woman, "notable among the apostles" (Rom. 16:7). In what sense Junia was "notable" or whether she was considered an apostle has been debated, but "apostle" or "emissary" could clearly be used to describe people who were not numbered among the traditional twelve apostles.[57]

Classical scholar Catherine Kroeger addresses the issue from the vantage point of "the socio-religious world of [Greco-Roman] women." Paul's congregations in Asia Minor, particularly Antioch, "lay in the very heart of Anatolia, where religious expression–particularly that of women–took on an extremely noisy, wild and orgiastic aspect." Citing the oppression and repression of women, Kroeger concludes, "In [religious ritual] they vented violent emotions that were not able to be expressed through any other channel ... Neither is it surprising that women who lacked any sort of formal education flocked to cults that were despised by the intellectuals."[58] In Greek sacrificial rites animals "were killed to the piercing cry of female spectators."[59]

By the end of the 1st century (at the latest), the official Christian view of women sounded "substantially the same as the pagan critique"[60]–"I do not permit a woman to teach or exercise authority over a man" (1 Tim. 2:12), and "the women must keep silent in the churches" (1 Cor. 14:32). In an almost comic reversal from female leadership to female submission, a late pseudo-Pauline letter describes younger women as horny, lazy, and subjects of scandal:

> Besides, [younger widows] get into the habit of being idle and going about from house to house. And not only do they become idlers, but also busybodies who talk nonsense, saying things they ought not to. So I counsel younger widows to marry, to have children, to manage their homes and to give the enemy no opportunity for slander. Some have in fact already turned away to follow Satan. (1 Tim. 5:13-15)

Christian opinion of women came to approximate educated pagan opinion. After noting that "women have often been the agents of possession" from a cross-cultural perspective, Maurizio summarizes various scholarly views, including "possession as a way for women to gain access to areas from which they are otherwise excluded." One such area was the exercise of religious power, "as long as they are believed to be possessed and to speak with the authority of the spirits"[61] that possess them. Similarly, in a study of the role of women in Old Testament divination, Homori notes, "it is common for interpreters to ascribe less agency to the [female] medium than the text does."[62]

As they set about correcting Mark's flaws, the authors of Matthew and Luke introduced a number of contradictions. Matthew appropriates the youth's words from Mark (Matt. 28:5-7), but in his revision the women are not struck dumb with fear. Rather, they run joyfully to inform the apostles that Jesus has risen and are met by Jesus on the way (Matt. 28:9-10). His expansion has the eleven remaining apostles go to Galilee–contradicting Acts 1:4 where the disciples are ordered to remain in Jerusalem. In Galilee the risen Jesus commissions the disciples to convert all the nations, but, we are told, *some doubted* (Matt. 28:17).

The Narrative Shifts

The doubt of some of the apostles clearly troubled the early church because, as Paul explained to the Corinthians decades before the gospels were composed, the resurrection of Jesus was already the keystone in the arch of his gospel. By the time the gospel of John was composed, the doubt of *some* has been reduced to the doubt of *one*, Doubting Thomas. "The doubt found in the Synoptics and associated with the appearance stories has been transferred from the women and the disciples as a group to Thomas as an individual."[63]

When Jesus proposes a trip to Bethany, the home of Lazarus, Thomas says, "Let us also go, that we may die with him" (John 11:16). The reference is ambiguous; is Thomas proposing that they will die with Jesus or with Lazarus? If, as I among others have suggested, the resurrection of Lazarus prefigures Jesus' own resurrection,[64] the ambiguity may be deliberate.

In any case, there is a clear narrative shift in terms of witnesses:

- A movement away from a few female witnesses to a larger group of male witnesses, and
- A corresponding movement away from a group of doubters to a solitary doubter.

Instead of relying on a single witness–Mary Magdalene, who mistakes Jesus for the gardener (John 20:14-15)–the stories move to a gathering of disciples (John 20:19-20). No longer is there a general disbelief–"they did not believe the women, because their words seemed to them like nonsense" (Luke 24:11). All the disbelieving is done by a single disciple, Thomas, who is commanded, "Stop doubting and believe!" (John 20:27).

Matthew, with "his known partiality for the sensational and miraculous"[65] doesn't even pretend to create a historical report. A story of an angel and an earthquake (Matt. 28:2) is followed by a ludicrous tale of *Roman* soldiers reporting to *Jewish* authorities who urge the soldiers *to tell their commander* that Jesus' "disciples came during the night and stole him away while we were asleep" (Matt. 28:11-13). One wonders what consequences lay in store for Roman soldiers *who confessed to sleeping on their watch* while a gang of Galilean rustics stole the corpse they were guarding. And if the soldiers were paid a hefty sum not to reveal what had happened (Matt. 28:15), "how did the real story leak out?"[66]

At the moment of Jesus' death, Matthew informs us,

> the curtain of the temple was torn in two from top to bottom. The earth shook, the rocks split and the tombs broke open. The bodies of many holy people who had died were raised to life. They came out of the tombs after Jesus' resurrection and went into the holy city and appeared to many people. (Matt. 27:51-53)

It's anyone's guess how the holy people "raised to life" the moment Jesus died on Friday passed their time until they emerged from their tombs on Sunday "after Jesus' resurrection." Mine is that they may have spent the intervening days playing the ancient game of knucklebones. After all, the bench tombs of the era generally contained multiple bodies and skeletal remains would have been plentiful.

Other admittedly less creative solutions have been proposed. One response intended to dispense with the bothersome phrase proposes that "after his resurrection" is an interpolation, a gloss inserted into the text at some point after its composition. Predictably, biblical literalists have rejected this face-saving scheme while suggesting that "their resurrection was intended to serve as a kind of testimony to the Jerusalemites"[67] who condemned Jesus and delivered him up to Pilate.

To the unconverted mind, the ultimate testimony to the "Jerusalemites" would have been *the appearance of the Risen Jesus Himself* rather than the creation of a dubious account of a swarm of holy zombies. But as we are oft-times reminded, God works in ways mysterious.

When Luke set about removing the last vestige of doubt about Jesus' return from the dead, he created another startling narrative shift. The appearances of the risen Lord begin to take on characteristics of classic ghost stories.

Deborah Thompson Prince, who has published a detailed comparison of the features of Luke's resurrection accounts with the features of classical ghost stories, concluded that "the method at work in Luke 24 is an attempt to disorient the reader in order to reconfigure the traditions known to the author and reader in light of the disciples' extraordinary experience of the resurrected Jesus."[68] She cites a number of examples of ghosts that were corporeal "revenants," capable of changing appearance at will, exhibiting a well-known spectral tendency to polymorphism, and engaged in various physical activities, including sexual intercourse. However, it seems to me Prince's conclusion that Luke is "disorienting" his readers is an attempt to rescue the resurrection "traditions" from being categorized as folklore.

Prince's conclusions risk blurring the question of how perplexing ghost stories were to the ancients–they were extraordinary by definition, hence their collection in the *paradoxa*, anthologies of weird tales. And were the ancients really any less confused than moderns when ghosts exhibited contradictory traits, being in some way physical yet defying the everyday laws of physics? Regarding the ghosts of Egypt, Adams notes, "Textual allusions or inferences would seem to point in favor of both of these visible types of manifestations of the dead [*spirit* and *shadow*] as being totally human in form."[69] Human in form, no doubt, but distinctly not-like-us in abilities.

Prince's claims, which are limited to the gospel of Luke, have predictably provoked an apologetic response. Jake O'Connell, then a student at Catholic Assumption College, published an attempted rebuttal in a periodical issued by McMaster Divinity College, a Baptist seminary. At the beginning of his piece, O'Connell concludes that "it is much more probable that Luke is not addressing Greco-Roman conceptions of apparitions at all; rather the similarities and differences are purely coincidental." But, he notes, "the same logic could be used to argue that all Christian accounts of the resurrection intentionally draw on Greco-Roman apparition types."[70] And that is basically the logic of the argument I intend to make, focusing specifically on the text of Luke and John.

O'Connell concedes that the various spectral characteristics cited by Prince "apply not only to Luke's resurrection appearances, but in varying degrees, to the appearances in Matthew, Mark, John and Paul as well; John in fact attests to all six of them." Consistently applying Prince's argument "leads to the conclusion that Matthew, Mark, John and Paul were intentionally invoking these models."[71]

Before briefly unpacking O'Connell's assertions, I would first point out that in the earliest and presumably most reliable manuscripts of Mark there are *no* post-mortem appearances. That is the problem posed by Mark's gospel in its earliest form, and also an obvious reason both for its expansion by the addition of spurious endings and the composition of resurrection stories by the other Synoptics and John.

In support of Prince's contention I would add two further observations. First, the appearances of Jesus in the resurrection stories share another trait often seen in ghost stories–the appearances are of *brief duration* during which admonition is provided or a message conveyed. Second, to quote Gabriel Hermon, who specializes in ancient social history, "would-be visionaries experience discomfort, isolation and incertitude,"[72] and if there is one feature on which the resurrection stories are consistent it is the distress and incertitude of the disciples.

Of course, the gospel writers need not have been "intentionally invoking" Greco-Roman folklore to produce their accounts, deliberately plagiarizing material from pagan sources. The minor inconsistencies between Jesus' post-mortem apparitions in the gospels and ancient ghost stories are easy enough to understand if one assumes the authors were borrowing–consciously or unconsciously–features of universally current ghost lore to flesh out their narratives. If, however, the gospel authors were cribbing from external sources to construct their "many convincing proofs" (Acts 1:3), one might at least grant that they were clever enough to recast the material. Nearly any undergraduate plagiarist might be assumed equally capable.

In either case, the elements of ghost stories are both "memorable and consequently repeatable," to say nothing of persistent. The popular image of the haunted house–large, dilapidated, remote, and connected with tragic death–has remained essentially unchanged for over two thousand years,[73] and any author, ancient or modern, could have easily recalled these features from memory.

As far as the influence of folklore on religion is concerned, the assumed oral transmission of the story of Jesus' life, prior to anyone writing it down for *at least a generation after the fact*, follows the same trajectory as folklore generally: "handed down ... from one person to another, repeated as it has been received and remembered and retold, [acquiring] a cultic character and function [while retaining] a magico-religious content and purpose."[74]

Even the New Testament writers' citations of the Old Testament are less than careful. Paul states that Jesus was "raised on the third day according to the Scriptures" (1 Cor. 15:4), but he doesn't cite any scripture, and what he had in mind is a matter of scholarly debate. Matthew says Jesus' family returned to Nazareth from Egypt so that "he would be called a Nazarene" (Matt. 2:23), supposedly according to the prophets, but refers to "a passage from a prophetic oracle that is nowhere to be found in the Scriptures."[75]

Ghost lore can certainly be summoned to support religious beliefs. During the English Reformation, "Catholic intellectuals called upon evidence from popular folklore about ghosts and visitations" to support the Church's teaching on Purgatory–"where else could ghosts have returned from but purgatory?"[76]

Lastly, as O'Connell notes, "Jesus' eating does not clearly separate him from non-bodily ghosts."[77] For ghosts to be perceptible, either visually or audibly, to ordinary waking consciousness presumes some element of physicality. It also assumes ghosts could appear from nowhere, eat, and then disappear.

That is demonstrated conspicuously by Phlegon's story of Polykritos, a man who returns from the dead on the occasion of the ill-omened birth of his hermaphroditic child:

> The people had clustered together and were arguing about the portent when the ghost took hold of the child, forced back most of the men, hastily tore the child limb from limb, and began to devour him . . . he consumed the entire body of the boy except for his head, and then suddenly disappeared.[78]

Greco-Roman lore widely assumes ghosts had appetites. If not, why the *eudeipnia*, or "suppers" that "are otherwise used only to describe offerings made to appease the souls of the dead" and libations poured at graves, offerings of "honey, milk, water, wine, or oil"?[79] Ritual feeding of the dead "was a common practice in the ancient world,"[80] as corroborated by the Old Testament–"I have not eaten any of the sacred portion while I was in mourning . . . nor have I offered any of it to the dead" (Deut. 26:14). Food left for the dead, including "bowls for foodstuffs, jugs for liquid," and knives are abundantly represented in ancient Judean graves.[81] The ghosts of heroes were offered the blood of jugulated animals, the blood flowing into a *bothros*, a trench prepared for the purpose.[82]

On the Road to Emmaus

The longest of the gospel resurrection stories is the "road to Emmaus" narrative. Two disciples meet a stranger to whom they relate the account of the women at the tomb. As they travel, Jesus (who they have been prevented from recognizing) explains the Old

Testament prophecies relating to himself. Finally, they eat the evening meal together, and the disciples receive a fleeting glimpse of the real Jesus when he blesses the bread, breaks it, and hands it to them. His appearance then comes to this jarring conclusion: "Their eyes were opened and they recognized him and he became invisible to them" (Luke 24:31).[83]

It's notable both that the disciples have heard the women's report of the empty tomb "but they are not convinced,"[84] and that their *failure to recognize Jesus on sight* is a reverse miracle of sorts, contradicting the very logic of his post-mortem appearances.[85] The account is meant to prove the reality of Jesus' resurrection, yet "the disciples themselves are under the force of some strange supernatural power" that prevents the "active recognition of [Jesus'] presence."[86] Dale Allison points out the contradiction inherent in the story "if one stresses the bodily continuity between the pre- and post-Easter Jesus" and yet the disciples fail to recognize him, concluding, "This is truly peculiar."[87]

Here is the account from Luke 24:2-30:

> "The chief priests and our rulers handed [Jesus] over to be sentenced to death, and they crucified him; but we had hoped he was the one who was going to redeem Israel. And what is more, it is the third day since all this took place.
>
> In addition, some of our women amazed us. They went to the tomb early this morning but didn't find his body. They came and told us that they had seen a vision of angels, who said he was alive. Then some of our companions went to the tomb and found it just as the women had said, but they did not see Jesus."
>
> He said to them, "How foolish you are, and how slow to believe all that the prophets have spoken! Did not the Messiah have to suffer these things and then enter his glory?" And beginning with Moses and all the Prophets,

he explained to them what was said in all the Scriptures concerning himself.

As they approached the village to which they were going, Jesus continued on as if he were going farther. But they urged him strongly, "Stay with us, for it is nearly evening; the day is almost over." So he went in to stay with them. When he was at the table with them, he took bread, gave thanks, broke it and began to give it to them. Then their eyes were opened and they recognized him, and he disappeared from their sight.

They asked each other, "Were not our hearts burning within us while he talked with us on the road and opened the Scriptures to us?"

They got up and returned at once to Jerusalem. There they found the Eleven and those with them, assembled together and saying, "It is true! The Lord has arisen and appeared to Simon." Then the two told what had happened on the way, and how they recognized Jesus when he broke the bread.

Prince, in a further interrogation of the Lukan account, notes "the rhetorical strategy" of the writer. The gentile author, who likely composed his work in Asia Minor late in the 1st century, "was aware of the scrutiny that such wondrous events elicited." Luke's rhetorical question, ("Why do you seek the living among the dead?", 24:5) responds, in "light of widespread suspicion and confusion over Christian claims about Jesus and objections like those of Celsus," to "uncertainty within the [Christian] community and suspicion from without."[88]

That uncertainty arises from a simple fact in the gospels: According to the most primitive tradition, the disciples who went to the tomb "*did not see Jesus*" (Luke 24:24).[89] The *tactile* Jesus described by Luke and John (Luke 24:39, John 20:17, 27) is an attempt to "counter the idea that the risen Jesus was some type of ghost or phantom,"[90] which, given the belief in soul survival in the 1st century, might count as a *naturalistic* explanation.

In the ancient world, ghosts, magic, and invisibility were closely associated. Luke's gospel makes a direct mention of invisibility in connection with the resurrection—"he became *invisible* (*aphantos*) to them" (Luke 24:31)—the only occurrence of *aphantos* in the New Testament. The Greek magical papyri preserve this spell for invisibility: "Arise, daemon from the realm below... whatever I may command of you... in that way obey me... if you wish to become invisible, just smear your forehead with the mixture and you will be invisible for however long you want."[91] Invisibility extends not only "to ghosts and other apparitions" but to magicians such as Pancrates as well.[92]

Besides the reference to the "daemon from the realm below," which may easily have referred to a ghost, the wording of the spell— to become *invisible* (*aphantos*)—duplicates Luke's description of Jesus' sudden disappearance. The sudden departure of ghosts is well attested in sources both ancient and modern. Besides the example of Polykritos, Lucian's story of the ghost of Eucrates' wife, who returns from the dead to reclaim a golden sandal, ends abruptly when the household dog barks: "and she vanished because of the barking."[93] A "female figure" seen simultaneously by several witnesses at Hinton Ampner, an English estate famous for hauntings, abruptly disappeared when the cook "suddenly reentered the kitchen, prompting the woman in silks to vanish in plain sight." A similar sudden disappearance is told of the ghost of a nun in the infamous Borley Rectory, a ghost that abruptly "vanished into thin air."[94]

Luke was not unaware of the ghostly nature of the Emmaus story. Indeed, the next incident he relates appears designed specifically to prove that Jesus is not merely a ghost:

> But while they were talking about these things he stood in their midst and said to them, "Peace be with you!" But they were alarmed and became afraid, thinking they were

seeing a spirit. And he said to them, "Why are you terrified and why do doubts arise in your hearts? Touch me and see, because a spirit does not have flesh and bones as you see I have." And saying this, he showed them his hands and feet.

But even in their joy they did not believe him, and while they were wondering he said to them, "Do you have anything here to eat?" And they gave him a piece of fish and he took it and ate it in front of them. (Luke 24:36-43)

Jesus proves his reality to his disbelieving disciples by having them touch him and by eating food in their presence, but the disciples wonder, as well they might, how a body of apparent flesh and bone has suddenly appeared from nowhere and requested a baked fish. It's worth noting, however, that ghosts *were* generally assumed to get hungry; the Roman poet Ovid, a contemporary of Jesus, advised Romans celebrating the Feralia, the day that ended Parentalia, "to leave their offerings on potsherds in the middle of the road" for the spirits "wandering around and consuming the food left for them."[95]

A similar case of corporal sensibility that is more apparent than real is related in Apuleius' story of the miller slain by a crone who turns out to be a ghost.[96] As Daniel Ogden observed, "The fact that the ghost could touch the miller's arm suggests that it had a solid form, but the fact that it could then disappear from a locked room suggests, perplexingly, that by contrast it was ethereal."[97] Finucane cites the ghost of Anchises, who invites his son to visit him in Elysium, and having issued the invitation, "the ghost vanished 'like vapour, into empty air.'"[98]

After analyzing the features of the Emmaus story, Ehrhardt concluded, "I believe that it is a serious error of modern theologians that they try to treat the recorded events of the first Easter as forming a coherent historical report. At any rate, the attempts to do so which I have seen, none of them, reached any convincing results."[99]

"A ghost does not have flesh and bones"

"Look at my hands and my feet! It's really me! Touch me and see, because *a ghost* (*pneuma*) does not have flesh and bones as you see I have" (Luke 24:39).

As noted by Daniel Smith, "no source in Jewish or Christian Greek before Luke uses [*pneuma*] for 'ghost.'"[100] Despite that fact, as Smith acknowledges, *pneuma*, *spirit*, is used in the magical papyri with the clear meaning of *ghost*: "grant me power over the spirit of this man who died a violent death."[101] Smith points out that the spirit of Jesus in Luke is not, however, raised as a result of necromantic ritual, i.e., Jesus is not "conjured up"[102] as described in the magical texts. Be that as it may, ancient sources are clear that ghosts could appear for their own purposes without being evoked.

The 4th century church historian Eusebius quotes an ancient variant of Luke's fish story: "He said, take, touch me and see that I am not a disembodied daemon (*daimonion asōmaton*)..."[103] "Daemon" is a common term for *ghost* or *spirit* in the magical texts and literature of the era. Lucian considered them commonplace, asking rhetorically whether "many others" hadn't "met with spirits (*daimonsin*), some at night, some during the day."[104]

In the Christian context, this use of *daimon* might reflect the belief that ghosts were evil spirits pretending to be souls of the dead. In any event, the version quoted by Eusebius is of great antiquity. An epistle by Ignatius, written at the beginning of the 2nd century, preserves it verbatim:

> For I know and believe him to have been in the flesh after the resurrection when he came to those with Peter and said to them, "Take, touch me and see that *I am not a phantom without a body*," and immediately they touched

him and believed … but after the resurrection he ate and drank with them as made of flesh, although spiritually united with the Father."[105]

Ignatius' explanation hardly clears up the ghostly nature of the risen Jesus, who is both "as of flesh" and "spiritually united with the Father," leaving us to suspect that Ignatius is having his cake and eating it too. Regardless, the disembodied daemon version "is clearly a free saying with a long history" known to Ignatius, Jerome–who believed it came from the now lost *Gospel According to the Hebrews*–and Origen, who cites it in the Latin version: "*Non sum demonium incorporeum*." Riley concludes, "Both Luke and Ignatius have drawn on a common source. Their source sought to demonstrate a material resurrection body by means of physical proof."[106] The ultimate source and history of this interesting variant remain conjectural, but leaves us with an unanswered question: *Whatever happened to the spirit known to Paul?*

Paul is clear that Jesus was raised "a life-giving *spirit*" (1 Cor. 15:45). "Now the Lord is *the Spirit*" (2 Cor. 3:17) and "even though we have known Christ according to the flesh, yet now we know Him in this way no longer" (2 Cor. 5:16). If "flesh and blood cannot inherit the kingdom of God" (1 Cor. 15:50), then presumably neither can "flesh and bones." Robinson proposed that the post-resurrection appearances diverged along two differing trajectories and that the quasi-physical, tactile manifestations of the later gospels "are secondary to an original luminous visualization of Christ's appearances" and that the path leading to the Apostle's Creed, which affirms belief in the resurrection of the body, "expressed the reality of the bodily resurrection by emphasizing, in spite of supernatural vestiges, the human-like-us appearance of the resurrected Christ: the resurrection of the *flesh*."[107]

"Though the doors were locked"

Significantly, Jesus' appearances tend to occur at night or toward the evening,[108] i.e., "between times" typically associated with hauntings and works of sorcery. It's a common observation in the literature on ghosts that their appearances occur at certain times, seasons, or places. *Liminal* times and places, doors, rivers, crossroads, dawn, dusk, and other changes of the light, as well as the transition from sleep to the waking state, are suited to the manifestation of souls caught between life and death.[109]

It is also clear from the frequent mention of lamps in the magical papyri that night was the propitious time for both magic and the appearance of ghosts. On this feature of the magician's work, Eitrem noted:

> The night with its horde of dead spirits and eerie ways–the night through which the sun god navigated in his vessel to reach the east through the dark kingdom of the underworld while the moon shone or the heavens were starry–offered the magician the best opportunity for exercising his art or arts."[110]

The nocturnal workings of the magicians were in large part a simple matter of physiology: "In general the association between sleep, death, dreams, and night was tight."[111] Matthew, for instance, clearly believed that at least some dreams were of supernatural origin (Matt. 2:12, 19). The world of the New Testament, a world before the ubiquitous glow of artificial light nearly banished darkness, was a world pullulating with works of sorcery. Ancient sources preserve terms such as *nuktiplanos*, "roaming by night," and *nuktoperiplanētos*, "wandering around by night," to refer to the activities of magicians as well, no doubt, of ghosts. The Dionysiac festivals and private mysteries "take place at night,"[112] and the magician practiced "the initiation rites, the migratory life, the nocturnal activities."[113]

Jesus' nocturnal manifestations in the gospel of John–"in the evening of the first day of the week" (John 20:19)–exhibit several spectral qualities. Jesus appears twice in the disciples' midst even though "the doors were locked" (John 20:19, 26). That "ghosts display a particular interest in doors"[114] is multiply attested by sources both ancient and modern. Apparently a high level of interest or even anxiety attended doorways; the Romans had no less than three minor deities concerned with doors: Cardea, the goddess of hinges; Forculus, the god of the door itself; and Limentinus, the god of the threshold.

Spirits haunted doorways and the ancients took precautions–"the threshold, or the vicinity of the door, was the place for performing all sorts of magic rites, which are, in the last analysis, generally concerned with the spirits of the dead," and "nails torn from graves and fastened to the threshold" have special protective powers.[115] "At the door the souls have one of their habitual haunts,"[116] an ancient and widespread belief that goes some way toward explaining the profusion of superstitions involving doorways. The door as the home of spirits may account for the bizarre ritual that confirmed a slave's refusal of manumission–"take an awl and push it through his earlobe into the door, and he will become your servant for life" (Deut. 15:17).

An extensive survey of apparitional experiences done by the Society for Psychical Research in the late 19th century recorded a number of cases in which "phantasms" of the recently dead appeared to have moved through locked doors.[117] The Society reported other cases in which apparitions moved about at will, touched the percipient, were seen simultaneously by another witness, or appeared to "fade away."[118] In every case reported by the Society, the person who saw the ghost was completely convinced of its reality and in every case the person seen as a ghost was confirmed to have died. The Society's working theory at the time seems to have been that the apparitions represented particularly vivid cases of telepathy between the living and the dying.

The Greek text of John uses the verb *kleiō*, "to lock," from *kleis*, "key." Translations that render the verb as simply *to shut* fail to convey the (miraculous) fact that the doors were locked, not simply closed, and that in spite of the doors being locked, Jesus "came and stood in their midst." Ancient critics of Christianity such as Porphyry found it odd that Jesus could walk right through locked doors but needed an angel to roll away the stone sealing the tomb.[119]

> So being the evening of that day, the first day of the week, and the doors having been locked where the disciples were for fear of the Jews, Jesus came and stood in their midst and said to them, "Peace to you!" and having said this, showed his hands and side to them. Consequently the disciples rejoiced because of seeing the Lord.
>
> And after eight days his disciples were again indoors and Thomas was with them. Jesus came, the doors having been locked, and stood in their midst and said, "Peace to you!" ... then he said to Thomas, "Put your finger here, and look at my hands, and reach out your hand and stick it into my side, and be not unbelieving, but believing."
>
> Thomas exclaimed, "My Lord and my God!"
>
> Jesus said to him, "You have seen me and believed. Happy are those who not having seen yet believe!" (John 20:19-21, 26-29)

Doubting Thomas has become the paradigm of unbelief, and that reveals the apologetic intent of the gospel accounts. Those stories would have little need of the profusion of such marvelous supernatural details as walking through locked doors and displaying pre-mortem wounds had Jesus' resurrection not already been the subject of doubt.

Doubt and disbelief within the early house churches would also account for editorial manipulation of the stories: "This motif of doubt is limited by John to the figure of Thomas alone: neither Mary nor the other disciples doubt ... The risen Jesus addresses Thomas alone, as though he had heard invisibly the conversation with his fellow disciples a week before."[120]

Fear, confusion, and doubt form a continuous thread connecting the resurrection stories:

> Trembling and bewildered, the women went out and fled from the tomb. They said nothing to anyone, because they were afraid. (Mark 16:8)

> When they saw him, they worshiped him; but some doubted. (Matt. 28:17).

> But they did not believe the women, because their words seemed to them like nonsense . . . He said to them, "Why are you troubled, and why do doubts rise in your minds? (Luke 24:11, 38)

> [Thomas] said to them, "Unless I see the nail marks in his hands and put my finger where the nails were, and put my hand into his side, I will not believe" . . . "Stop doubting and believe." (John 20:25, 27)

Jesus the Revenant?

The post-mortem apparitions of Jesus in Luke and John exhibit traits of the *revenant*, a semi-embodied ghost that appears once or for a short time following the death of the subject[121] and performs bodily functions such as speaking, eating, and displaying the wounds that ended life.[122] I use the term "*semi*-embodied"; even though Jesus is tangible, a locked door poses no barrier to his entry and although seemingly solid, he can suddenly disappear. The Jesus of the gospels of Luke and John displays other behavior typical of ghosts: "late classical tradition attributed various activities to ghosts, such as informing, consoling, admonishing, and pursuing the living."[123]

Vermeule's observation is particularly pertinent to the post-mortem Jesus of the gospel of John: "wounding the flesh means wounds in the shade below."[124] "That Jesus as a ghost would appear with wounded side, hands and feet, was what would have been expected in his culture. So John adds the demand of Thomas to touch Jesus, the one thing reputed to be impossible in the Greco-Roman tradition concerning the souls of the dead."[125]

Saint Peter Attempting to Walk on Water[126]

However, ancient tradition was not unanimous that ghosts were intangible, as the legend of Philinnion proves. In any case, the display of the wounds that ended life is typical of ancient ghosts. The ghost of Sychaeus displays the wounds of the dagger that killed him to his sister Dido–"the ghost of her unburied husband came to her in dream: lifting his pale head in a strange manner, he laid bare the cruelty at the altars, and his heart pierced by the knife"[127]–and in the same poem the bloody ghost of Hector appears, "showing his wounds."[128]

It was widely believed in Jesus' era that certain classes of the dead, "well-defined categories of restless death,"[129] were particularly likely to come back as ghosts: the prematurely dead, the unmarried, and the executed. According to the gospel evidence, Jesus, like his predecessor John the Baptist, could be numbered among all those groups that shared commonalities identified by Sarah Johnston, those "unable to pass into death because they were not really finished with life," as well as one other essential trait: "It was not so much the *violence* of a death that causes a ghost to walk, as it is the *reason for* or the *mode of* death that makes a difference. Most important, *dishonorable* deaths are problematic."[130]

Crucifixion, considered a most dishonorable form of execution, was reserved for slaves and the lowest of criminals. So, based on widely held 1st century beliefs, Jesus possessed all the essential requirements of an angry, restless ghost: a violent, premature, dishonorable death. Little wonder the gospel writers were at such pains to prove that Jesus was not merely an apparition.

It's probably significant that the Greek of Luke's gospel reflects a higher social register than that of either Matthew or Mark. The historiographic preface to Luke's gospel (Luke 1:1-4), in keeping with official histories of the era, "indicates that the author has done extensive research."[131] If that was indeed the case, it was quite likely the author was familiar with accounts of ghosts in secular histories as well as the popular *paradoxa*, collections of fantastic and bizarre events that quite naturally included ghost stories.

Phlegon of Tralles' tale of the recently dead Philinnion, who repeatedly returns from the grave to have sexual relations with her family's guest Machates, has several features in common with the apparitions of Jesus that are, for lack of a better word, uncanny. Like Jesus, Philinnion appears at night–"night came on and now it was the hour when Philinnion was accustomed to come to him"– and like Jesus in the Emmaus narrative, "she ate and drank with [Machates]."[132] After her panic-stricken parents interrupt her tryst, she upbraids them: "how unfairly you have grudged me being with the guest *for three days*," and then succumbs once again to death.[133] When the thoroughly rattled citizens investigate this amazing occurrence, they find Philinnion's tomb empty, but containing tokens of affection gifted her by Machates.

The shared elements of the stories include:

1. The empty tomb,
2. Tokens left behind by its former occupant–in the case of Jesus, burial wrappings (John 20:5-7),
3. The shock and awe experienced by witnesses (Mark 16:8),
4. Eating and drinking as "proof of life,"
5. The evening appearances of the revenant, and
6. The passage of three days.

To assume that the shared similarities of these short narratives are mere chance, accidents of free composition, amounts to conjuring up a supernatural set of coincidences by the power of wishful thinking. They become easily comprehensible, however, when you allow that the gospel writers may have drawn upon a fund of shared cultural assumptions about how ghosts behave. The tokens left in the tomb, linen cloths in Jesus' case, "makes it clear that it was the same body that was buried which rose from the dead."[134]

Sexual attraction between ghosts and the living is reflected in a fragment of an ancient novel included among the Greek magical papyri which alludes to a "handsome phantom" (*kalon eidōlon*) that appears to a woman.[135] Evidently, she was only one of many enamored of, um, a "phantastic" body.

Spirit intercourse with humans is accepted in the New Testament as well: "the holy spirit will come upon" Mary (Luke 1:35) and she will conceive. Sexual interaction with spirits was well known in the wider culture as well, evidenced by Origen's claim that Apollo's spirit entered the priestess through her vagina (*Contra Celsum* VII, 3), a claim his Christian audience evidently found completely credible. There was also the story of Philinnion, who returns each night from her grave to have sex with Machetes. Paul intended to present his followers as "a pure virgin" to the Risen Christ who will be their "husband" (2 Cor. 11:2). And mystical union with the divine, expressed in terms of sexual symbolism as well as the lore of the succubus and incubus, are so well known that they require no further comment.

By describing the woman who was the primary witness of Jesus' resurrection as *hysterical* (*paroistros*),[136] Celsus appears to imply a sexual component to her reaction. A related term, *oistraō*, is used by Lucian to describe a man turned into a donkey by magic as acting, "like a man *mad with lust* (*oistroumenos*) for women and boys."[137] "The hysterical female, Mary Magdalene, fits the image of the woman susceptible to bizarre religious impulses that emerges from ancient literature.

Yet she is by no means a silent victim of Jesus' magic. "Although deluded by sorcery, Mary Magdalene also becomes one of the main perpetrators. She is an active witness, a creator of the Christian belief in the resurrection."[138] The gospel of Mark implies that Mary Magdalene, from whom seven demons had been expelled (Mark 16:9), was a bit more than slightly out of the ordinary.

Ancient accounts of the disappearance and reappearance of the famous dead is hardly limited to the story of Jesus. Here, according to Plutarch, is how the career of Romulus was reported to have ended:

> Romulus was perceived to transform suddenly, and no part of his body or shred of clothing was seen. Some speculated that the senators, gathered in the temple of Haphaistos, rose up against him and killed him, and distributed pieces of his body to each to carry away hidden in the folds of his clothing. Others believe it was neither in the temple of Hephaistos, nor when the senators alone were present that he disappeared, but when he held an assembly around the so-called Marsh of the Goat. Suddenly wonders strange to describe occurred

IV: THE RESURRECTION AS GHOST STORY

in the air, incredible changes, the light of the sun faded and night fell, not gently or quietly, but with terrible thunder and gusts of wind driving rain from every direction, during which the great crowds scattered in flight, but the influential men huddled together with one another.

When the tempest had passed and the sun broke out and the mass reassembled, there was an anxious search for the king, but the men in power neither inquired into the matter nor investigated it, but loudly exhorted all of them to honor and worship Romulus as a man imbued with divinity, a god favorably disposed to them rather than a worthy king. The mass of people, believing these things, left rejoicing with high hopes to worship him. However some bitterly contested the matter in a hostile way and accused the patricians of foisting a stupid story on the people, being themselves the perpetrators of murder.

At this point, a man from among the patricians, high born, reliable and most esteemed, a trusted intimate of Romulus himself, a colonist from Alba, Julius Proculus, went into the forum and swore by the most sacred emblems that as he traveled along the road he saw Romulus approaching him face to face, handsome and strong as ever, decked out in bright, shining armor. He himself, struck with fear at the sight, said, "O king, what were you thinking, subjecting us to unjust and evil accusations, the whole city an orphan in tears, weeping for having been abandoned?"

Romulus answered, "It pleased the gods, Proculus, that I be with men for just so long a time, and having founded a city of superlative glory, dwell again in heaven. Farewell, and proclaim to the Romans that if they practice self-control with manliness, they will achieve the very heights

> of human power. And I will be your propitious daemon, Quirinus."
>
> Based on the character of the man who related them, and because of his oath, these things seemed believable to the Romans, besides feeling some participation in divine destiny equal to possession by the gods. No one objected, but all set aside suspicion and opposition and prayed to Quirinus, calling upon him as a god.
>
> . . .
>
> Romulus is said to have been fifty-four years old, in the thirty-eighth year of his rule when he disappeared from among men. [139]

If Luke sought, consciously or not, to imitate the genre of the classical ghost story or other fabulous "histories" in framing his accounts of Jesus' post-resurrection appearances, his technique might have at the very least set a precedent that the author of John then followed. Alternatively, and in my view far less feasibly, it's possible that the gospels of Luke and John were not influenced by Greco-Roman literary conventions. In that case, we are confronted with a primitive New Testament tradition that contains examples of independently drawn ghost stories.

I am the Translation and the Life

However, the account of Romulus is not, strictly speaking, a resurrection story. Rather, it is a *translation fable*. Notable figures who are "translated" do not die and rise again but are suddenly taken up to heaven.[140]

Perhaps the best-known translation story in the Old Testament is Elijah's ascent in a chariot of fire—"As they were walking along and talking together, suddenly a chariot of fire and horses of fire appeared and separated the two of them, and Elijah went up to heaven in a whirlwind . . . And Elisha saw him no more" (2 Kings

2:11-12). Other figures from the Old Testament are also taken up: "Enoch walked faithfully with God; then he was no more, because God took him away" (Gen. 5:24).[141]

Richard Miller has made a carefully argued case that "prevailing scholarship regarding Mark's enigmatic ending may prove nothing short of delusional" and that the abrupt ending may instead represent a "Hellenic convention ... a hybridic literary work" consistent with a "broader systemic literary context," in which the gospel's much-debated ending can be correctly understood.[142] Miller cites Plutarch's *Life of Romulus* and notes, "Hellenistic and Roman literature is replete with translation fables commonly indicated by the disappearance of the deified hero."[143] He also notes the examples of Herakles, Amphiarus, Diomedes, Oedipus, and Castor and Pollux, as well as a number of lesser-known figures.[144] Similarly, Leipoldt refers to the case of Apollonius of Tyana, whose career "comes to an end with a kind of ascension into heaven. He enters the temple and vanishes."[145]

Daniel Smith has also made a case that the abrupt ending of Mark is "a post-mortem disappearance narrative,"[146] but prefers the term "assumption" instead of "translation." Smith cites a number of similarities between the empty tomb story in Mark and ancient translation or assumption accounts: the disappearance, the absent body, the fruitless search, and an epiphany at a distance,[147] all of which are features of the Romulus story.

Smith also references the *Gospel of Peter* that says Jesus ascended from the cross.[148] Following the lead of earlier scholars, he observes that, strictly speaking, "a resurrection may only be proved by narrating either an encounter with the risen person or the event itself. Mark 16:1-8 does neither."[149]

Remember, in the canonical gospels *nobody* actually witnesses the risen Jesus leave the tomb. It could even be argued that Jesus' ascension to heaven occurs in stages. He says "into your hands I entrust my spirit" (Luke 23:46) at the moment of his death, but "I have not yet ascended to the Father" (John 20:16) after his resurrection.

Although Prince asserts that burial would "immediately set aside an expectation of a translation story,"[150] an *initial* burial might have been understood as necessary to harmonize the account with proof texts in the Hebrew scriptures:

> Seeing what was to come, [David] spoke of the resurrection of the Messiah, that he was not abandoned to the realm of the dead, nor did his body see decay. (Acts 2:31).

> What God promised our ancestors he has fulfilled for us, their children, by raising up Jesus. As it is written in the second Psalm: "You are my son; today I have become your father." God raised him from the dead so that he will never be subject to decay. (Acts 13:32-34)

Prince's reading would, it seems to me, also assume that Luke and John understood the true intention of Mark's ending, if Mark indeed intended it as a translation story. Alternatively, the other gospel writers may have correctly understood Mark's intention to create a translation story, but changed it to a resurrection story to reflect the theology current in their day.

For Prince's point to stand up under scrutiny, it also seems that one must "subsume Mark under a Judaic literary domain,"[151] i.e., discounting the possible influence of Greco-Roman translation lore. Additionally, Miller cites the transfiguration that features the previously translated Elijah ("there appeared before them Elijah and Moses," Mark 9:4) as "prefiguring the translation of Mark's protagonist. Mundane bodies are not raised but are translated into bodies similar to those of 'the angels of heaven.'"[152] Paul insists on the same point in 1 Corinthians 15: they are "sown a natural body, and *raised up a pneumatic body*."[153] Whatever the intention of Mark, it is clear the gospel accounts, then as now, are open to multiple interpretations, or as an apologetic writer admits, "an unlimited number of possibilities."[154]

Another account with similarities to the gospels concerns the wonder worker, Apollonius of Tyana, who urged his friends to distance themselves from him while he awaited trial before the paranoid Emperor Domitian, but to expect his reappearance.

> "Alive," asked Damis, "or how?"
>
> "As I myself believe, alive, but as you will believe, risen from the dead."

After Apollonius reappears, still alive, this is the reaction of his disciples:

> Whereupon Apollonius stretched out his hand and said, "Take hold of me and if I evade you, then I am indeed a ghost come to you from the realm of Persephone... but if I resist your touch, then you shall persuade Damis also that I am both alive and that I have not abandoned my body." They were no longer able to disbelieve, but rose up and threw themselves on his neck and kissed him.[155]

The gospel of John implies that Jesus could disappear at will, a trait shared by Apollonius. After the healing at Bethzatha, Jesus "slipped away into the crowd" (John 5:13), and when the authorities sought to arrest him, Jesus "eluded their grasp," or literally "went out from their hand" (John 10:39). After a debate in the Temple, "[the authorities] tried to seize him, but no one laid a hand on him, because his hour had not yet come" (John 7:30). Compare this to Apollonius, who after proclaiming that he was not yet destined to die, "disappeared from the courtroom."[156] and during his hearing before Domitian, makes a slyly mocking reference to the ability of magicians to break out of bonds: "If you think me a wizard, how will you ever fetter me? And if you fetter me, how can you say that I am a wizard?"[157]

The gospel tradition that Jesus appeared post mortem in various forms is an additional point of interest. Besides his appearance on the road of Emmaus (Luke 24:15-16), he appears on the shore of the Sea of Galilee, again initially unrecognized (John 21:4). At the tomb, Mary Magdalene at first mistakes Jesus for the caretaker (John 20:15). Following these leads, the apocryphal gospels and acts of the 2nd century will add additional appearances of Jesus in the form of a boy, a youth, an old man, or in the form of Paul or Andrew or Thomas. "The world of the apocryphal acts . . . is, in many ways, the Hellenistic world in which magic and sorcery were quite at home."[158] Shape-shifting, or *polymorphy*, is a well-recognized ability of ancient ghosts.[159]

According to Origen, Jesus was polymorphic even in life: "Jesus, being one, had more than one reflection and to those who saw him he did not appear in the same way . . . he was not always present nor did he appear even to the apostles themselves . . . before his Passion he was clearly visible to the multitude, although not always, but before his Passion he no longer appeared in the same way."[160] Lalleman points out that "Polymorphy in the narrow sense is not found in the texts that are older than the [Acts of John] and the [Acts of Peter] (2nd century AD),[161] but notes a tradition of shape-shifting in the spurious ending of Mark: "Afterward when two of them went walking in the country, he appeared in another form" (Mark 16:12).

Apologist scholars have proposed a number of supposedly objective criteria by which the resurrection stories can be positively judged as representing historical fact, but as Avalos points out in a devastating critique, the very same criteria could be applied with positive results to full-bodied apparitions of the Virgin Mary.[162] Oddly enough, no evangelical scholars seem to take such sightings seriously although many hundreds of witnesses over the course of centuries have testified to the reality of such appearances.

That the infancy narratives of Matthew and Luke are fictional concoctions motivated by apologetic intent is widely recognized in mainstream New Testament studies. I would argue that the post-mortem appearances of Jesus, particularly in Luke and John, are also amalgamations fabricated from widely known and readily available cultural lore available to the gospel writers. The gospel writers had plenty of material to work with, given all the stories circulating about revenants–full-bodied apparitions of the recently dead, tangible and capable of performing the functions of the living.

Jesus, executed as a dishonored criminal, presumably unmarried and childless, and dead before the natural span of life, represents a perfect candidate for a restless ghost with magical powers. On the possibility that Jesus remained unburied, a further precondition of the restless ghost is met: "The [*atelestoi* or "uncompleted"] are the dead that have not received the due rites. Such spirits, like the ones of those who have died by violence or before their time, cannot achieve rest."[163]

Every essential feature of the resurrection stories–sudden appearance and disappearance, the fear and confusion of witnesses, the empty tomb and tokens found within it, speaking, eating, and drinking as proof of life, tangible presence, the brevity of the appearances, the display of pre-mortem wounds, encouraging and admonishing–is also found in contemporary Greco-Roman ghost stories. Luke, writing a minimum of fifty years after the events of Jesus' life, had a rich cultural repertory of legends and popular ghost lore from which to construct the details of his resurrection narratives as well as an abundance of motive to do so. Prince's contention that the details of Luke's resurrection narrative are drawn from ghost lore is thoroughly credible.

Similar analysis, based on texts unrelated to the gospels, offers these observations on material that crosses genres, observations that merit some extensive quoting from Winkler. A "narrator whose purpose is fundamentally religious," he says, "may make use of story patterns from popular tales" including "oral folk-narrative," reproduction of narrative structure "does not entail a direct literary dependence." Narrative, says, Winkler,

> is not a privileged art–either as technique or possession–but a freely circulating system of uncopyrighted themes and combinations. Narrators make free use of what they

> find effective in capturing an audience… an author might make use of standard thrilling situations from popular narrative and also invest them with a religious meaning.[164]

A case in point is the Angels of Mons legend that began during the First World War. According to witnesses, soldiers at risk of death, supernatural reinforcements variously identified as "French cavalry," "the bowmen of Agincourt," and "a whole choir of angels," appeared and saved the hard-pressed British troops. The story was popularized by one Arthur Machen, "an occultist with a deep interest in Celtic and Welsh mysticism, and an accomplished writer of fiction."[165]

Similar battle apparitions are known from the classical literature, particularly the battle of Marathon that later became the site of a famous and dangerous haunting. Forty-nine instances of battlefield apparitions are known "for ancient Greece alone," leading to the conclusion that they and similar "sensed presences" are due to "a psychological mechanism built into human nature."[166] In any case, "an integral part" of battle apparitions and the Wild Hunt of European legend appears to be "the collecting of souls of those who have died violently."[167]

Besides the doubt simmering within the early Christian community, the resurrection proved unbelievable to many potential converts as well: "When they heard Paul speak about the resurrection of the dead, some laughed in contempt" (Acts 17:32). Both the Jewish community and the early Christian movement included adherents who were believers but denied resurrection on principle: "Then the Sadducees, who say there is no resurrection, came to him with a question" (Mark 12:18). Paul's insistence on the centrality of the resurrection also strongly implies that some within his churches doubted it or interpreted it differently: "how can some of you say that there is no resurrection?" (1 Cor. 15:12). Celsus knew of some Christian sects that rejected "the doctrine of the resurrection according to scripture."[168]

The writers of the gospels had compelling motive to create and then further embroider resurrection narratives. There were defects of the primitive tradition that relied on female witnesses of dubious reliability finding an empty tomb. There was doubt from both within and without the early Christian communities. And there were competing theologies to contend with.

They also had an abundance of popular folklore from which to draw–consciously or not–the elements of their stories as a comparison of the gospels with surviving ghost lore demonstrates. "Christian theology could hardly have developed in a vacuum unaffected by the styles and modes of thought of the late pagan world."[169]

One further motive for the manufacture of appearance stories must not be overlooked. The "occurrence of epiphanies is often conducive to the creation of power bases that serve a clever elite well."[170]

Back to Celsus

Celsus must be explicitly acknowledged as the first to raise the issues of witness reliability *and* psychology as an explanation for the resurrection accounts:

> While [Jesus] was alive he did not help himself, but after death he rose again and showed the marks of his punishment and how his hands had been pierced. But who saw this? A hysterical female, as you say, and perhaps some other one of those who were deluded by the same sorcery, who either dreamt in a certain state of mind and through wishful thinking had a hallucination due to some mistaken notion (an experience which has happened to thousands), or, which is more likely, wanted to impress the others by telling this fantastic tale, and so by the cock-and-bull story to provide a chance for other beggars.[171]

This is an early example of "the context of suspicion and the adversarial mindset" of the "elite levels of Greco-Roman society" with its expectations for "authors to support fantastic narratives with strong evidence and a plausible argument."[172] Curiously, advocates of the current "social-scientific perspective" seem to universally overlook Celsus' opinion. Craffert, quoting another author with approval, claims that "the vision-as-delusion view is culturally insensitive (ethnocentric) and 'entirely inappropriate for the ancient Mediterranean world.'"[173] Celsus and the multitude of Jesus' other ancient Jewish and pagan critics would no doubt be quite surprised to find that their opinions didn't represent the "ancient Mediterranean world."

In fact, there were likely *many* in the ancient world who doubted that "visions are as real as what is experienced in waking consciousness."[174] Those who adhere to the "social-scientific perspective" may be the ones guilty of insensitivity to the spectrum of ancient opinion: "Since these people lived by a different logic and consensus reality [the resurrection] was neither a mere delusion nor objectively real, but culturally real."[175]

I seriously doubt that any early Christian who accepted the doctrine of the bodily resurrection thought of it as anything other than "objectively real," or that the Christian sects known to Celsus who rejected the resurrection thought of it as anything more than "mere delusion." Moreover, it is obvious that many in the ancient world were no more credulous than moderns.

Lucian, for example, was completely aware of religious fraud; it is the subject of his *Lover of Lies*, *On the Death of Peregrinus*, and particularly his *Alexander the False Prophet*. Lucian describes Alexander's machinations so well that modern writers detect in Alexander the traits now associated with malignant narcissism: grandiosity, sexual predation, and lack of empathy. Narcissism "often plays a role in the origins of religion or in the motivation for religious leaders within existing traditions."[176]

On the resurrection as ghost story specifically, Celsus maintained that Jesus appeared to his disciples afterwards "like a ghost hovering before their perception."[177] Celsus' vocabulary, if accurately quoted, suggests the drifting of something insubstantial before one's vision.

Celsus, who "demonstrated a particularly keen acquaintance with Christian sacred writings,"[178] is essentially unknown except for the tendentious quotations preserved in Origen's *Contra Celsum*, an attempted refutation of Celsus' work written decades after he had died. Celsus, writing eighteen centuries ago, was the first to equate the gospel resurrection accounts with ghost stories, anticipating by many centuries the conclusion, "it would have been extraordinary *if there were no apparitions* of Jesus to some of his companions after his death." But "apparitions of Jesus do not constitute resurrection. They constitute apparitions, no more and no less."[179]

Of all the diseases sent by the gods in antiquity, "madness is the most frequent."[180] It appears that nothing much has changed in that regard since the days of Celsus.

Notes

1. Kirby, *Journal of Higher Criticism* 9 (2002) 184.
2. Ibid, 184.
3. Lincoln, *Journal of Biblical Literature* 108 (1989) 289.
4. Goulder, *Journal for the Study of the Historical Jesus* 3 (2005) 191.
5. Burkill, *Numen* 3 (1956) 161.
6. Nodet, *Biblica* 91 (2010) 348. (My emphasis.)

    "The Markan tradition (followed by Matthew and Luke) is quite clear that Jesus' last meal was a Passover celebration . . . John, however, is equally clear that Jesus died the day *before* the Passover." Bond, *The Historical Jesus*, 148.

7. Burkill, op. cit., 164.
8. Kennard, *Journal of Biblical Literature* 74 (1955) 228.
9. Burkill, op. cit., 168.

10. Kodell, op. cit., 19.

11. Ibid, 21.

12. Riley, op. cit., 1.

13. *Polycarp to the Philippians* 7:1-2.

14. Matthew 21:42-44, 26:14-15, Luke 19:41-44, John 1:11, 12:37-38, 19:13-15, for example.

15. Herman, op. cit., 152.

16. Wernik, *Numen* 22 (1975) 96-130.

17. Spilka et al., op cit. 6-7.

18. 1 Thessalonians 1:10, Romans 4:24, Galatians 1:1, etc.

19. Allison, op. cit., 229

20. Cheek, op. cit., 193.

21. Riley, op. cit., 106.

22. Allison, *Resurrecting Jesus*, 200, 215.

23. Snape, *Numen* 17 (1970), 194.

24. Marshall, *Tyndale Bulletin* 24 (1973) 66-72, 77.

25. Kirby, *Jesus Beyond the Grave*, 233.

26. Lecouteux op. cit., 15.

27. Kennard, *Journal of Biblical Literature* 74 (1955), 235.

28. Lowder, op. cit., 262.

    However, as Helen Bond points out, "the very existence of a formal, fixed Jewish council known as *the* Sanhedrin has been repeatedly called into question in recent years . . . The most up-to-date research suggests that the High Priest alone made all the decisions." *The Historical Jesus*, 156.

29. Snape, op. cit., 194-95.

30. Miller, *Journal for the Study of the Historical Jesus* (2011) 87-88.

31. Teeple, *Journal of Biblical Literature* 89 (1970) 56-57, 61.

32. Shannon, *Working Papers on Nervan, Traganic and Hadrianic Literature* 1.9 (2013).

33. Kennard, op. cit., 227, 233.

34. Miller, *Journal of Biblical Literature* 129 (2010) 767.

35. Crossan, *Who Killed Jesus?,* 160-61, 183.

36. Conner, *Magic in Christianity: From Jesus to the Gnostics*, 289-94.

37. Allison, op. cit., 202. See also Richard Carrier, *Journal of Higher Criticism* 8 (2001) 304-18.

38. Fuhrmann, *Policing the Roman Empire*, 187.

39. Most authorities put the date of composition somewhere between 80-110 CE.

40. Scroggs & Groff, *Journal of Biblical Literature* 92 (1973) 535.

41. Vermeule, *Aspects of Death in Early Greek Art and Poetry*, 21.

42. David, *Religion and Magic in Ancient Egypt*, 84.

43. Pickup, *Journal of Evangelical Theological Studies* 56 (2013) 522-542.

    The spirits of the dead "were thought to linger near their graves." Janowitz, *Icons of Power: Ritual Practices in Late Antiquity*, 85-95.

44. Riley, op. cit., 8.

45. "According to Mark the resurrection appearance is to take place in Galilee and according to Matthew it actually does... according to Luke the appearances all take place in Jerusalem and its neighborhoods, and appear to be concentrated into one day." Marshall, *Tyndale Bulletin* 24 (1973) 56.

46. "Resurrection appearances had to have been made in a *highly charged apocalyptic context* where the end was imminent and God's power was at the point of breaking into the world... These hopes and expectations... presumably stoked the flames of an existing and evolving eschatological fervour." Bond, *The Historical Jesus*, 173.

47. Mark 8:31-38, 9:30-32, 10:32-34.

48. Plevnik, *Biblica* 61 (1980) 500.

49. Kannaday, op.cit., 141.

    As Johnston trenchantly observes, "fantastic occurrences" are religion if wrought by the gods or men but magic if wrought by women. *Restless Dead*, 33-34.

50. Setzer, *Journal of Biblical Literature* 116 (1997) 259.

    In connection with the Corinthian practice of "baptism on behalf of the dead" (1 Cor. 15:29), DeMaris remarks, "Funerary rituals in Greco-Roman society were overwhelmingly in the hands of women" *Journal of Biblical Literature* 114 (1995) 680.

51. Chadwick, *Origen: Contra Celsum*, 109 (II, 55).

52. Lane Fox, *Pagans and Christians*, 310.

53. MacMullen, *Christianizing the Roman Empire (AD 100-400)*, 39.

54. Irwin, *Journal of the American Society for Psychical Research* 87 (1993) 6-8.

55. Kelly, *Journal of Parapsychology* 75 (2011) 310, 316.

56. 1 Corinthians 3:5, 2 Corinthians 3:6, for example.

57. 1 Corinthians 4:6, 9, Philippians 2:25, for example.

58. Kroeger, *Journal of the Evangelical Theological Society* 30 (1987) 25, 26, 28.

59. Lane Fox, op. cit., 70.

60. Setzer, op. cit., 271.

61. Maurizio, *Journal of Hellenic Studies* 115 (1995) 75.

62. Hamori, *Journal of Biblical Literature* 132 (2013) 834.

63. Riley, op. cit., 94.

64. Conner, *The "Secret" Gospel of Mark*, 124-41.

    Compare Riley, *Resurrection Reconsidered* (118): "Lazarus is the only one dead at the time, and is the referent of the pronoun 'him' . . . Thomas suggests that not only is Lazarus not going to be raised, but that he and his fellow disciples are going to die along with him."

65. Wenham, *Tyndale Bulletin* 24 (1973) 21.

66. Wenham, op. cit., 23.

67. Quarles, *Journal of the Evangelical Theological Society* 59 (2016) 276.

68. Prince, *Journal for the Study of the New Testament* 29 (1987) 297.

69. Adams, *Current Research in Egyptology 2006*, 3

70. O'Connell, *Journal of Greco-Roman Christianity and Judaism* 5 (2008) 191-92.

71. Ibid, 194.

72. Herman, op. cit., 145.

73. Felton, op. cit., 1, 38-39.

74. James, *Numen* 9 (1962) 4.

75. Nodet, *Biblica* 91 (2010) 206.

76. Bennett, *"Alas, Poor Ghost!"* 140 (online).

77. O'Connell, op. cit., 196.

78. Hansen, *Phlegon of Tralles' Book of Marvels*, 30-31.

79. Johnston, op.cit., 41, 223.

    "Take this libation and these clippings of hair, and go to Clytemnestra's grave. Stand there and pour this mixture of honey, milk and wine over the grave . . ." Euripides, *Orestes*, 112.

80. Bar, *Biblica* 91 (2010) 269.

81. Bloch-Smith, op. cit., 218.

82. Brown, *Greek, Roman, and Byzantine Studies* 23 (1982) 311-12.
83. The breaking of bread has Eucharistic overtones that are examined in a later chapter.
84. Ehrhardt, *New Testament Studies* 10 (1964) 188.
85. Alter, *The Resurrection: A Critical Inquiry*, 538.
86. Howe, *Journal of the Evangelical Theological Society* 18 (1975) 173.
87. Allison, op. cit., 227.
88. Prince, *Journal of Biblical Literature* 135 (2016): 123-24, 134.
89. Compare Mark 16:6, "he is not here."
90. Riley, op. cit., 53.
91. Preisendanz, op. cit., I, 14.
92. Pease, *Harvard Studies in Classical Philology* 53 (1942) 6, 22.
93. Lucian, *The Lover of Lies*, 27.
94. Clarke, op. cit., 41, 252.
95. Dolansky, op. cit., 132.
96. Apuleius, *Metamorphosis* IX, 29-31.
97. Ogden, *Night's Black Agents*, 70.
98. Finucane, op.cit., 21.
99. Ehrhardt, *New Testament Studies* 10 (1964) 193.
100. Smith, *Catholic Biblical Quarterly* 72 (2010) 756.
101. Betz, *The Greek Magical Papyri in Translation*, 72 (IV, 1950-1951).
102. Smith, op. cit., 759.
103. Eusebius, *Ecclesiastical History* III, 36.
104. Lucian, *The Lover of Lies*, 17.
105. Ignatius, *Ad Smyrnaeos*, 3. (" . . . a phantom without a body," following Lake's translation, *The Apostolic Fathers*).
106. Riley, *Resurrection Reconsidered*, 95-96.

    The history of the variant is contested and, in the final analysis, probably untraceable. Mitchell, "Bodiless Demons and Written Gospels," *Novum Testamentum* 52 (2010) 221-40.
107. Robinson, *Journal of Biblical Literature* 101 (1982) 16.
108. Matthew 28:1, Mark 16:2, Luke 24:29, John 21:4.
109. Felton, op. cit., 93-95.
110. Eitram, *Magika Hiera*, 176.

111. Ogden, *Greek and Roman Necromancy*, 77.

112. Burkert, *Greek Religion: Archaic and Classical*, 291.

113. Luck, *Witchcraft and Magic in Europe: Ancient Greece and Rome*, 104.

114. Clarke, op. cit., 14.

115. Ogle, *American Journal of Philology* 32 (1911) 254-255.

    The tomb itself is a threshold, a doorway of sorts: "because of the presence of these spirits of the dead the threshold, like the cross-roads, was a spot peculiarly adapted to the performance of magic rites, just as such rites were often performed on graves." Ogle, *American Journal of Philology* 32 (1911) 270.

116. Riess, *American Journal of Philology* 17 (1896) 191.

117. Gurney, et al., *Phantasms of the Living*, Volume I, 102, 436, 448.

118. Ibid, 400, 435, 438, 445-446, 448.

119. Grant, *The Journal of Religion* 28 (1948) 189. Compare Matthew 28:2.

120. Riley, op. cit., 103, 119.

121. Evans, *Field Guide to Ghosts*, 19.

122. Lecouteux: "the wound that has been inflicted upon the revenant can be found on it when its grave is opened." *The Return of the Dead*, x.

123. Finucane, op. cit., 25.

124. Vermeule, op. cit., 49.

    "Greek ghost beliefs generally assume some connection between the state of the body and the state of the ghost." Johnston, *Restless Dead*, 158.

125. Riley, op. cit., 117-118.

126. François Boucher, 1766.

127. Vergil, *Aeneid* I, 355.

128. Ibid, II, 270.

129. Ogden, *In Search of the Sorcerer's Apprentice*, 117.

130. Johnston, op.cit., 149.

131. Ehrman, *The New Testament*, 115.

132. Hansen, *Phlegon of Tralles' Book of Marvels*, 26.

133. Ibid, 27.

134. Robinson, *Journal of Biblical Literature* 101 (1982) 12.

135. Preisendanz, op. cit., 20-21.

136. Origen, op. cit., II, 55.

137. Lucian, *Lucius or The Ass*, 33.

138. MacDonald, *Early Christian Women and Pagan Opinion*, 124.

139. Plutarch, *Lives* I, 27.5-28.3, 29.7.

140. Pease, *Harvard Studies in Classical Philology* 53 (1942) 1.

141. For the disappearances of Enoch, Elijah and Moses, see Tabor, *Journal of Biblical Literature* 108 (1989) 225-38.

142. Miller, *Journal of Biblical Literature* 129 (2010) 759-61, 770.

143. Ibid, 764.

144. Ibid, 764-66.

145. Leipoldt, *Journal of Higher Criticism* 4 (1997) 741.

146. Smith, *Novum Testamentum* 45 (2003) 128.

147. Ibid, 128-32.

148. *Gospel of Peter* 5:19.

149. Smith, op. cit., 130.

150. Prince, op. cit., 296.

151. Miller, op. cit., 759.

152. Luke 20:36, for example.

153. Miller, op. cit., 769.

154. Cheek, op. cit., 199.

155. Philostratus, *Life of Apollonius of Tyana*, VII, 41, VIII, 12.

156. Philostratus, *Life of Apollonius*, VIII, 5.

157. Ibid, VII, 34.

158. Goldin, *Aspects of Religious Propaganda in Judaism and Early Christianity*, 167-68.

159. Felton, op. cit., 85.

160. Origen, *Contra Celsum* II, 64-66.

161. Lalleman, *The Apocryphal Acts of John*, 111.

162. Avalos, *The End of Biblical Studies*, 191-94.

163. Ogden, *Witchcraft and Magic in Europe: Greece and Rome*, 22.

164. Winkler, *The Journal of Hellenic Studies* 100 (1980) 156-57, 165.

165. Clarke, op. cit., 217.

166. Herman, *Historia: Zeitschrift für Alte Geschichte* 60 (2011) 140.

167. Houston, *Western Folklore* 23 (1964) 158.

168. Origen, op.cit., V, 12.

169. Finucane, op.cit., 30.

170. Herman, op. cit., 130.
171. Chadwick, op. cit., 109 (II, 55).
172. Prince, *Journal of Biblical Literature* 135 (2016) 129-30.
173. Craffert, *Journal for the Study of the Historical Jesus* 7 (2009) 144.
174. Ibid, 146-47.
175. Ibid, 147.
176. Kent, *Ancient Narrative* 6 (2007) 78, 86, 89, 95.
177. *Contra Celsum* VII, 35. My translation of *phasma hōsperi pararreusanta pros to ophthēnai autois*.
178. Kannaday, *TC: A Journal of Biblical Textual Criticism* 11 (2006) online.
179. Crossan, *Neotestamentica* 37 (2003) 47.
180. Smith, *Transactions and Proceedings*, 411.

V

The Resurrection as Magic

> For as often as you eat this bread and drink the cup, you proclaim the Lord's death until He comes.
>
> —1 Corinthians 11:26

A Christ with Calories

Historian Dale Allison said it as well as anyone: "Of all the things that the New Testament is clearly mistaken about, the most obvious is its conviction, plainly expressed in a good number of places, that the consummation is near to hand." He cites the three predictions in Revelation–"Behold, I am coming soon!" (Revelation 22:7, 12, 20)–as failure to return as promised. A forged letter of the apostle Peter "knows of 'scoffers'" who ask, "Where is this 'coming' he promised?" (2 Peter 3:4) and "John 21:22-23 reflects consternation that the Beloved Disciple has died even though Jesus has not returned."

Allison also points to the plain meaning of Mark 9:1, "There are some standing here who will not taste death until they see that the kingdom of God has come with power." He concludes, "Somebody reasonably enough understood this or something like it to mean that not all of Jesus' disciples would die before the consummation."[1]

Kodell draws attention to the emergence of Eucharist theology during a period "marked by a growing awareness of the delay of the parousia" and the realization that "many [believers] would die before the end," an impression "confirmed by the death in the 60s of the great leaders, Peter, Paul, and James."[2] The expectation of an imminent apocalypse "was certainly the oldest [interpretation], and remained a determinative view until near the end of the [first] century when its importance declined due to a rising interest in universalistic and ecclesiastical ideas."[3]

I find Maccoby's brief summary of Jesus' probable beliefs convincing on both historical and textual grounds: "Jesus' scenario of the future contained the Jews as the people of God, restored to independence in their Holy Land, and acting as a nation of priests for the whole world in the Kingdom of God."[4] Apocalyptic belief is the "oldest distinguishable level" of Christian doctrine and "remained a determinative view until near the end of the [first] century."[5]

Multiple New Testament passages show that the arrival of the Kingdom was initially understood to be imminent. The End was considered so close that those married were to live as if celibate–"the appointed time has grown very short. From now on, let those who have wives live as though they had none" (1 Cor. 7:29). The general resurrection would take place in the very generation that heard Jesus preach these urgent words:

> The men of Nineveh will stand up at the judgment with *this generation* and condemn it; for they repented at the preaching of Jonah, and now something greater than Jonah is here. The Queen of the South will rise at the judgment *with this generation* and condemn it; for she came from the ends of the earth to listen to Solomon's wisdom, and now something greater than Solomon is here. (Matt. 12:41-42)

Jesus even predicted that his disciples would not finish preaching to Israel before the Son of Man arrived–"Truly I tell you, you will not finish going through the towns of Israel before the Son of Man comes" (Matt. 10:23).

There was a tight connection between the Last Supper and the coming Kingdom: "After taking the cup, he gave thanks and said, 'Take this and divide it among you. For I tell you *I will not drink again from the fruit of the vine until the kingdom of God comes*'" (Mark 14:25). The earliest documents of the New Testament establish a clear link not only between Jesus' death and resurrection but also with his parousia:[6]

> *to wait for his Son from heaven,* whom he raised from the dead—Jesus, who rescues us from the coming wrath. (1 Thess. 1:10)

> For he has set a day when he will judge the world ... He has given proof of this to everyone by raising him from the dead. (Acts 17:31)

The institution of the Eucharist "was in part a response to the delay of the parousia." When Paul first linked the Parousia to the Eucharist—"you proclaim the Lord's death until he comes" (1 Cor. 11:26)—"expectation of the early return of the Lord was very much alive."[7] By the time Luke composed his gospel, late in the 1st century or at the beginning of the 2nd, hope for an imminent Parousia, the physical presence of Jesus, was fading fast and his post-mortem appearances had adjusted accordingly.

In the story of Jesus' manifestation on the road to Emmaus, "Jesus was recognized by them *when he broke the bread*" (Luke 24:35). The breaking of bread is a clear Eucharistic reference. Jesus is now recognized by a ritual gesture and not by his wounds. By the end of the 1st century the Eucharist had already become a placeholder, a proxy, for the much delayed Parousia—Jesus is now present *in flesh and blood* in the emblems of the Eucharist. In the mid to late 300s, Cyril of Jerusalem wrote that Jesus

> Himself declared and said of the Bread, This is My Body, who shall dare to doubt any longer? And since He has Himself affirmed and said, This is My Blood, who shall ever hesitate, saying, that it is not His blood? ... is it incredible that He should have turned wine into blood?[8]

Cyril's convictions aside, even the "Eucharistic words" of Luke's gospel are not above suspicion "of ideological alteration" as recent publications demonstrate.[9]

A frankly magical understanding of the Eucharist is apparent in the earliest documents of the New Testament. Those who eat without "recognizing the body" eat and drink their own condemnation. "That is why many of you are weak and sick and some have even died" (1 Cor. 11:30).

The Eucharist is magically transformed into the flesh of God, its power "released by the words of the celebrant. Once these words are spoken, the effect is permanent and the 'new' substance exists quite objectively or independently of the persons involved."[10]

"The central doctrine of the Eucharist which asserts that mere bread and wine are changed into the actual Body and Blood of Christ through the recitation of special words accompanied by prescribed gestures, belongs to the world of magic."[11] Smith remarks on "how perfectly crude" is Paul's attribution of "this magical effect" to the "misuse of the holy food."[12]

Food as a conduit for spiritual forces is well known in antiquity:

> Leave a little of the bread you did not eat, and breaking it apart, make seven morsels and go to where the heroes and gladiators and men who died violently were slain. Say the spell into the morsels and toss them.
>
> This is the spell to be pronounced into the morsels . . .[13]

Similarly, the piece of bread Jesus dips in the bowl and hands to Judas is the sign to the Adversary to approach and take control–"after the morsel, then Satan entered into him" (John 13:27). Ensorcelled food was only one of several means of magical transmission. Consider the following early Christian spell reproduced in Kotansky's *Greek Magical Amulets*:

> God of Abraham, God of Isaac and God of Jacob, protect Alexandra, daughter of Zoē, from demons and enchantments . . . lest you use potions on her, either by a kiss . . . *or by food, or by drink* . . . or by the evil eye, or by

an article of clothing... One God and his Christ, help Alexandra.[14]

Understanding the Eucharist as magic coheres with the pagan estimation of Christian ritual generally as "a magical movement pandering supernatural wonders." Its "exorcisms, glossolalia, healings, praying 'in the name of Jesus,' and making signs of the cross could all be viewed as magic."[15] I have argued elsewhere that the line between magic and religion is imperceptible,[16] and Chatley's *The Monist* (1908) shows that I'm hardly the first to make that claim: "[T]here is no essential difference between a religious man who prays for the recovery of one sick and the white magician who invokes good spirits to produce the same results."[17]

It is frankly impossible to reconcile the words of the Jewish law–"None of you may eat blood, nor may any foreigner residing among you eat blood" (Lev. 17:12)–with the notion of drinking Jesus' blood: "*Whoever feeds on my flesh and drinks my blood* has eternal life" (John 6:54). Certainly not with any exegetical laxity from the Jewish Jesus of Matthew, who proclaimed, "anyone who sets aside one of the least of these commands and teaches others accordingly will be called least in the kingdom of heaven" (Matt. 5:19). Maccoby:

> Such a concept of the death of Jesus cannot be reconciled with any variety of Judaism... The implication of the Eucharist that salvation is to be obtained through Jesus' death and the shedding of his blood is thus a radical departure from Judaism and a return to pagan concepts of atonement.[18]

The Jerusalem Council set forth "minimum legal requirements"[19] for gentiles joining the Christian movement. One of those requirements stipulated that they abstain "from the meat of strangled animals and from blood" (Acts 15:20).

Paul himself compares the Eucharist to pagan sacrifices:

> [T]he sacrifices of pagans are offered to demons, not to God, and I do not want you to be participants with demons. You cannot drink the cup of the Lord and the cup of demons too; you cannot have a part in both the Lord's table and the table of demons. (1 Cor. 10:21)

It's been suggested that the story of the Last Supper "is but an etiological cult story, analogous to the Greek myths or to the Hebrew fable of the Passover in Exodus [12], designed to authorize a custom otherwise established in the earliest community."[20] Whatever the case may be, "the association of wine and blood, especially around the Mediterranean where red wine predominates, is natural and is attested outside of Greece, in the Semitic realm."[21]

Most shocking of all from the pagan standpoint was the open Christian introduction of *theophagy*, the eating of a god—"whoever feeds on my flesh." The theology of the Eucharist almost certainly contributed to pagan claims that Christians practiced cannibalism. Early Christian writers seem to avoid the subject of theophagy, perhaps because "they had some feeling of a certain deep identity between the theophagy of the pagan myth and the Eucharist... Christianity made theophagy explicit in ritual and theology."[22] Absorbing the qualities of the victim consumed was essentially the theory behind ritual cannibalism.

By the end of the 1st century (at the latest), Christians had come to physically identify Jesus with God. Jesus' flesh became God's flesh and God's flesh became food. "The teaching of the Church is explicit on this point. The body eaten is the same as that once born of a virgin and now seated at the right hand of the Father."[23] The identification of Jesus with God may be reflected in a text as early as Acts: "Be shepherds of the church of God, which he bought with his own blood" (Acts 20:28).

The debate over this passage has been carried on "almost *ad nauseam*," but an argument can and has been made that at least by implication "it was by God's own blood that the Church was purchased."[24] When Ignatius writes his epistle to the Ephesians in the early 2nd century, he can speak of "Jesus Christ our God,"[25] speak of "the spark of life renewed by the blood of God,"[26] and famously call the Eucharistic bread, "the medicine of immortality, the antidote that we may not die."[27] It's almost certainly no coincidence that Eusebius uses identical language to describe Isis' discovery of "the medicine of immortality"[28] and her use of it to grant immortality to her son Horus.

By the time *1 Clement* is composed—one of the earliest Christian documents outside the New Testament—"let us gaze upon the blood of Christ"[29] has taken on the language of epiphany, the technical language for "gazing at God or for gazing at the divine."[30] Little wonder that by the Middle Ages the blood of Christ is invoked in magical grimoires: "I conjure thee by virtue of the blood of Jesus Christ contained daily in the chalice."[31]

The cross, too, had its magical powers: Tapping yourself four times on the torso in a cross-shaped sign, it was promised, "opens doors, quenches poisonous drugs and bites, drives out demons, hexes pagan sacrifices and oracles, foils all sorts of real magic and witchcraft, and even keeps tools sharp."[32]

Holy relics of wood and nails (multiplied as much as the loaves and fishes in all the claimed bits and pieces, of course) were also potent forces, and not just because they were supposedly from *Jesus'* cross; "iron linked with the dead, especially the blood of the criminal dead, was believed to possess special potency."[33] Accordingly, Lucian's Eucrates says, "The Arab gave me the ring made from the iron [nails] of crosses and taught me the spell of many names."[34] Coptic spells used by Christians invoke "the sufferings ... upon the cross" as well as "the wood of the cross."[35]

Quite naturally, receiving the emblems of the Eucharist also assumed magical power. The spells of sorcerers never work against Christians who have taken Communion and wear the cross, and "the instruments of the Passion" including "the Holy Sponge," the "Holy Cross," and even the "Holy Lance" accordingly make their way to Constantinople in 614.[36]

In the Name of Jesus Crucified

As we've seen, the theory of magic that was current in his era would have made the risen Jesus almost inevitably into a source of power by virtue of his untimely death. A curse from the magical papyri says of a ghost: "Osiris will grant your request because you are *untimely dead* (*aōros*) and childless and wifeless."[37] Assuming Jesus was unmarried, childless, wifeless, both dead before his time *and* by violence, he would have been the perfect candidate to join the ranks of the restless dead. Magical praxis included calling up ghosts to achieve a desired goal:

> I deposit [in a grave] this binding spell with you, underworld gods . . . and under-world ghosts, men and women dead before their time, virgins and youths . . . Kamēs, ghost of the dead, raise yourself for me, from the repose that holds you fast . . ."[38]

Both Jesus' spirit and the objects once related to him, particularly substances connected to his execution, became potent sources of magical energy. Miracle-working power adheres to things associated with the miracle worker, which is the obvious motive for the preservation of relics of saints.

The practice began early in Christianity, as evidenced by the collection of the bones of the martyred Polycarp–"So afterward we collected his bones, more valuable than the most precious stones, more excellent than gold, and put them aside for ourselves in a suitable place."[39] Christians and (other) magicians were notable for gathering up remains of the dead, and their doing so "was suspiciously like magicians' collection of the remains of bodies of executed criminals (the martyrs were legally criminals) whose spirits they wished to control."[40]

We hardly need to venture outside the pages of the New Testament to establish that *magical power resides in the names of the executed dead*. When Peter and John are arrested, their inquisitors ask, "By what power or what name did you do this?" (Acts 4:7). The answer has already been given:

> Jesus of Nazareth was a man accredited by God to you by miracles, wonders and signs . . . and you, with the help of wicked men, put him to death by nailing him to the cross. But God raised him from the dead. (Acts 2:22-24)

The raising of Jesus "is the foundation miracle for the whole narrative of Acts."[41] Having come proclaiming "the mystery of God," Paul was "resolved to know nothing while I was with you except Jesus Christ and him crucified . . . My message and my preaching were not with wise and persuasive words, but with a demonstration of the spirit's power" (1 Cor. 2:2-4). In his letter to the "bewitched" Galatians, "Jesus Christ crucified" supplies both "the spirit" and the resulting "performance of works of power" (Gal. 3:1, 5). The Ephesian Christians will know "the surpassing greatness of his power . . . which [God] put into operation by raising Christ from the dead" (Eph. 1:19-20).

It's abundantly attested that early Christians used the formula "in the name of Jesus Christ crucified" to perform their magic. The *Acts of John* includes an example: "I, John, command you in the name of Jesus Christ the crucified . . ."[42] Justin Martyr, describing the exorcisms of his day, says, "they are exorcized in the name of Jesus Christ, crucified under Pontius Pilate."[43] According to Paul, Jesus "was ordained the Son of God in power owing to the spirit of holiness by resurrection from the dead" (Rom. 1:4), and Jesus' death and resurrection are subsequently and inevitably adapted to magical ends as this example of spell working indicates:

> Christ was born. Amen
> Christ was crucified. Amen.
> Christ was buried. Amen.
> Christ was raised. Amen.
> . . .
> You, too, fever with chills,
> Flee from Kalēs who wears this magic charm.[44]

The Christian apologist Origen believed in the magical power of names, above all the name of Jesus: "demons and other unseen powers . . . fear the name of Jesus as superior" and the demons fly away "at the recitation of his name."[45] Origen's belief coincides exactly with the superstitious nonsense parodied by Lucian: "the fever or the swelling is in fear of a divine name and because of this flees from the inflamed gland."[46] Challenged by Celsus, Origen insists that Christians are not using incantations to expel demons. Rather, he says, they are exorcizing evil spirits

> by the name of Jesus, combined with recitals of the accounts about him, for recitation of these things has often succeeded in having driven the demon from men . . . indeed, the name of Jesus is so powerful against the demon that now and then it is effective even when named by unworthy men."[47]

Although Origen did not consider the use of Jesus' name *and other words in which exorcists had confidence* as magic, the modern scholar would certainly classify such "recitations" as examples of *historiolae*, "short stories recounting mythical themes"[48] designed to magically reproduce the miracles of the original story. Regarding the magical use of *historiolae*, Brashear observed,

> mythical events (archtypes) 'once upon a time' (*in illo tempore*) retain their supernatural forces forever and can

be reactivated at any given time by the simple act of recounting them ... the precedent having been cited, the god is obligated to act the same way now as then.[49]

Janowitz sums up Origen's belief about the power of names: "The power of a divine name is automatic and not based on the intention of the speaker."[50] "The spirits of the prophets are subject to the prophets" (1 Cor. 14:32) even as "the demons are subject to us in your name" (Luke 10:17).

In Origen's opinion, the names of divinities work due to "a certain mysterious divine science"[51] *because they are divine names*, Jesus' name above all because he has been given "the name above all other names" (Phil. 2:9). Therefore the difference between Christian magicians and pagan magicians is not the difference in their approach—"they use an identical method to address divine or daimonic powers and the only difference consists in the extent of their effect" and Christian incantations "take effect even in cases when the one who pronounces them is not aware of the meaning of the words."[52]

As Weltin pointed out, "our pagan would feel comfortably at home in his new [Christian] surroundings; in a familiar way he seemingly saw efficacy attaching to names, set words, and prescribed signs all used in a rehearsed way by the priest ... Undoubtedly his ingenuity was taxed to discover any objective differences between the good old pagan magic in the mystery religions and the new mystic efficacy in the Christian dispensation."[53]

Notes

1. Allison, op.cit., 113-15.

2. Kodell, *The Eucharist in the New Testament*, 83-84.

   "Death had become an eschatological problem in another connection. The death of believers before the Parousia had raised doubts and questions." Martin, *Scottish Journal of Theology* 17 (1964) 334.

3. Scott, op. cit., 19.

4. Maccoby, op. cit., 50.

5. Scott, op. cit., 19.

6. Beasley-Murray, op. cit., 296.

   Nevertheless it is clearly the case that "Jesus preached the coming of [the kingdom] of God, rather than his own return." Bond, *The Historical Jesus*, 146.

7. Kodell, op. cit., 121.

8. Cyril, *Fourth Mystagogic Cathechism*, IV, 22.

9. Epp, *Biblica* 90 (2009) 410.

10. Weltin, op. cit., 93.

11. Magoulis, *Byzantion* 37 (1967) 228.

12. Preserved Smith, *The Monist* 28 (1918) 188.

13. Preisendanz, op. cit., IV, 1392-95.

14. Kotansky, *Greek Magical Amulets*, 278-81.

15. Hartog, *The Routledge Companion to Early Christian Thought*, 60.

16. Conner, *Magic in Christianity*, vii-x.

17. Chatley, *The Monist* 18 (1908) 510-11.

18. Maccoby, op. cit., 110-111.

19. Achtemeier, *Catholic Biblical Quarterly* 48 (1986) 5.

20. Smith, *The Monist* 28 (1918) 178.

21. Burkert, *Homo Necans*, 224.

22. Herrero de Jáuregui, *Orphism and Christianity in Late Antiquity*, 355, 357.

23. Smith, *The Monist* 28 (1918) 161.

24. DeVine, *Catholic Biblical Quarterly* 9 (1947) 381.

25. Ignatius, *Ephesians*, Prœmium, 18.

26. Ibid, 1. My translation of *anazōpurēsantes en haimati theou*.

27. Ibid, 20. My translation of *pharmakon athanasias, antidotos tou mē apothanein*.

28. Eusebius, *Praeparatio Evangelica* II, 14.

29. *1 Clement* 7:4.

30. Fisher, *Vigiliae Christianae* 34 (1980) 221, 233.

31. Chatley, op. cit., 513. The quotation comes from the *Grimoire of Pope Honorius*.

32. Weltin, *Greek, Roman, and Byzantine Studies* 3 (1960) 79.

33. Alfayé Villa, *Magical Practice in the Latin West*, 441.
34. Lucian, *Lover of Lies*, 17.
35. Meyer & Smith, *Ancient Christian Magic*, 176, 178, 180.
36. Magoulias, op. cit., 239-240, 250-51.
37. Daniel & Maltomini, *Supplementum Magicum*, 52.
38. Kotansky, op. cit., 50.
39. *The Martyrdom of Saint Polycarp*, XVIII, 2.
40. Morton Smith, *Studies in the Cult of Yahweh*, II, 211.
41. Myllykoski, *Wonders Never Cease*, 162.
42. Daniel & Maltomini, op. cit., I, 95, quoting the *Acts of John*.
43. *Iustini Martyris Dialogus cum Tryphone*, 118.
44. Daniel & Maltomini, op. cit., 23.
45. Origen, op. cit., III, 36.
46. Lucian, *The Lover of Lies*, 9.
47. Origen, op. cit., I, 6.
48. Kotansky, *Magika Hiera*, 112.
49. Brashear, *Aufstieg und Niedergang der römischen Welt* II, 18.5, 3439.
50. Janowitz, *History of Religions* 30 (1991) 360-62.
51. Chadwick, *Contra Celsum* I, 24.
52. Šedina, *Listy filologické* 136 (2013) 22, 23.
53. Weltin, op. cit., 97.

VI
Wrapping Up

> This is an evil in all that is done under the sun, that there is one fate for all men.
>
> —Ecclesiastes 9:3 (NASB)

Christ raises Lazarus from his tomb[1]

Imagine that you have enrolled in a creative writing course. Today your instructor has given the class a new assignment: Write a story about a haunted house. What do you know about haunted houses? Quite a lot, it turns out.

The house is large, old, dilapidated, possibly remote. Most important, it has a tragic or sordid history. The house is connected to a murder, a mysterious disappearance, or some event even more horrific—a body buried in the basement, perhaps, or the victim of a madman immured alive within its walls.

Why is the house rumored to be haunted? People approach it with a sense of foreboding. Passersby glimpse figures looking down from the windows, even though it's thought to be abandoned. The otherwise talkative locals fall suddenly silent, changing the subject and exchanging looks freighted with significance whenever the place gets mentioned.

A person with no particular interest in ghost stories or the supernatural will nevertheless easily recognize these common elements of the haunted house tale. Even someone who has never read a ghost story will find them familiar, predictable, even trite. Assuming you're not a professional ghost hunter or an avid fan of uncanny stories, how do you know these details? The answer, of course, is obvious: You absorbed them, bit by bit, from the wider culture in the same way we all acquire a vast repertoire of cultural knowledge without being specifically taught it.

This process of imperceptible accretion occurs in all societies and has in all ages, past and present. Starting from earliest childhood, we all accumulate an immense store of culturally specific beliefs, mores, attitudes and information. We learn how to differentiate between what is said seriously, what is sarcastic, and what is said in jest. We catch tones and the connotations of our words, nuances that foreigners often miss, but we cannot generally explain exactly how we know these things or when we learned them. We know the elements of the haunted house story because everyone knows them. That's just how it is.

Everyone who has read the New Testament with the least attention knows that the writers make frequent reference to the Old Testament. Those who have read the New Testament more closely are aware the Old Testament pervades the New, that the references to the Old include not only specific quotations, but themes, story elements and even plot lines. Specialists know that the Old Testament quotations often derive from the Septuagint, the ancient Greek translation of the Old Testament. The Old Testament was an essential part of the culture of early Christianity and early Christian writers turned to it instinctively for proof texts,

VI: WRAPPING UP

for religious vocabulary, for explanations, and for solutions to theological problems.

In addition to their participation in the culture of Judaism and its scriptures, the New Testament writers were members of another culture as well, the wider Greco-Roman culture. Paul and the authors of the gospels spoke its language, lived in its cities, traveled its roads, observed its religious festivals and rituals, and likely absorbed common sayings from its works of literature.

When it came time to tell the central story of Christianity, to explain how and why a man came back from the grave, the New Testament writers used the only resources available to them: the language and frames of reference current in their culture–the culture of Judaism and the Old Testament, and the wider Greco-Roman culture in which Judaism was embedded. So it's hardly surprising that we've encountered visions in the New Testament similar to stories of visions from Greco-Roman sources, or that terms from the nearly ubiquitous mystery cults find their way into the letters of Paul and his imitators. That common elements of ghost lore should also appear in stories of Jesus, returned from the grave to make a brief appearance to his disciples, is less surprising still.

The only remaining question is why it has taken modern readers so long to suspect the source of these elements in the post-resurrection stories is Greco-Roman ghost lore. The most obvious reason is confessional allegiance. Christian believers have been assured from childhood that the stories of the New Testament are *sui generis*, utterly unique in that they were inspired by the Holy Spirit, and literally true, word for word. The notion that the resurrection accounts were cribbed, consciously or not, from the broader culture's understanding of death and survival after death would have been dismissed as ridiculous at best, blasphemous at worst.

And to expect that skeptics would have automatically overcome the barrier of confessional allegiance is to overestimate our ability to think originally. Most of us who now critically interrogate the text of the New Testament probably came from the ranks of believers; I can think of no convincing reason a non-believer would devote the time and effort necessary to engage with the New Testament on the level of original language or to read it closely enough to become suspicious of its claims. And finally becoming skeptical of New Testament truth claims does not confer some magical power to transcend the limitations of our previous belief. "Thinking outside the box" isn't as straightforward as it sounds when the "box" is the conditioning of an entire culture and the education behind an academic career.

A Personal Revelation

I distinctly recall when I realized that elements of the resurrection stories closely matched those of Greco-Roman ghost stories. For years, I had harbored no belief whatsoever in the resurrection, but seeing the connection still came as a bit of a shock. Even though I could find no corroborating opinion in the professional literature, the sheer numbers of close similarities nevertheless left me convinced, confident such parallels could not be coincidental, merely accidents of free composition. Some time later I learned that Celsus, who had not shared my cultural "box," had advanced the ghost story scenario centuries earlier.

Further reflection raised the question of where anyone would derive the details of a story of a man returned from the dead. Where indeed, other than the resources of the larger culture? Those who still cling to the belief that Jesus returned from the grave and appeared to his disciples must account for the various close parallels between the stories in Luke and John and Greco-Roman ghost lore generally. Believers in a literal resurrection (of some kind) might also explain, given modern psychological insights, how apparitions of Jesus differ in kind from modern apparitions of ghosts. After all, the main reason people believe in ghosts is that people keep seeing them.

So, as we have seen, there turns out to be very little "revelation" in "revealed" religions. Time after time it can be demonstrated that de novo "revelations" consist of elements borrowed from the wider culture. There's no wizard hiding behind the curtain, nor is one required. The stories of the resurrection, like your writing assignment about the haunted house, consciously or subconsciously tapped into story elements available in the ambient cultural environment, past and present. That the New Testament resurrection accounts have evaded this sort of analysis since the times of Celsus speaks more to our self-induced blindness than to the purported revelations of the gospels.

Notes

1. Etching by F. Ludy after J.F. Overbeck, 1849. From the Wellcome Collection, https://wellcomecollection.org/works/hfkejcbp.

References

Achtemeier, Paul J. "An Elusive Unity: Paul, Acts, and the Early Church," *Catholic Biblical Quarterly* 48 (1986) 1-26.

Adams, Christina. "Shades of Meaning: The Significance of Manifestations of the Dead as Evidenced in Texts from the Old Kingdom to the Coptic Period," *Current Research in Egyptology 2006*, M. Cannata, ed, 2007, Oxbow Books.

Aitken, Ellen Bradshaw. "[*ta drōmena kai to legomena*]: The Eucharistic Words in First Corinthians," *Harvard Theological Review* 90 (1997) 359-70.

Alfayé Villa, Silvia. "Nails for the Dead: A Polysemic Account of an Ancient Funeral Practice," *Magical Practice in the Latin West: Papers from the International Conference held at the University of Zaragosa 30 Sept.-1 Oct. 2005*, 2010, Brill.

Allison, Dale C. *Resurrecting Jesus: The Earliest Christian Tradition and Its Interpreters*, 2005, T&T Clark.

_. *The Historical Christ and the Theological Jesus*, 2009, William B. Eerdmans Publishing Company.

Alter, Michael J. *The Resurrection: A Critical Inquiry*, 2015, XLibris.

Alvarez-Rodriguez, Javier. "Psychic Neuronal Hyper-synchronies: A New Psychiatric Paradigm?" *Health* 6 (2014) 2089-99.

Aubert, Jean-Jacques. "Threatened Wombs: Aspects of Ancient Uterine Magic," *Greek, Roman, and Byzantine Studies* 30 (1989) 421-99.

Aune, David F. "Magic in Early Christianity," *Aufstieg und Niedergang der römischen Welt*, H. Temporini & W. Haase, eds, 2.23.2 (1980) 1507-57.

Avalos, Hector. *The End of Biblical Studies*, 2007, Prometheus Books.

Bagnani, Gilbert. "'Sullani Manes' and Lucan's Rhetoric," *Phoenix* 9 (1955) 27-31.

Bar, Shaul. "The Oak of Weeping," *Biblica* 91 (2010) 269-74.

Bauckham, Richard. "The Women at the Tomb: The Credibility of their Story, *The Laing Lecture at London Bible College*. (online)

Beare, Frank W. "Concerning Jesus of Nazareth," *Journal of Biblical Literature* 87 (1968) 125-35.

Beasley-Murray, George R. "Resurrection and Parousia of the Son of Man," *Tyndale Bulletin* 42 (1991) 296-309.

Bennett, Gillian. "'Alas, Poor Ghost!" Case Studies in the History of Ghosts and Visitations," *University Press of Colorado, Urban Institute*, 1999, online.

Berkey, Robert F. "[*ENGIZEIN, PHTHANEIN*], and Realized Eschatology, *Journal of Biblical Literature* 82 (1963) 177-87.

Bertram, George. "[*energeō*]," *Theological Dictionary of the New Testament*, G. Kittel, ed, 1964, William B. Eerdmans.

Betz, Hans Dieter. *The Greek Magical Papyri in Translation Including the Demotic Spells*, 2nd ed, 1992, University of Chicago Press.

Bloch-Smith, Elizabeth M. "The Cult of the Dead in Judah: Interpreting the Material Remains," *Journal of Biblical Literature* 111 (1992) 213-24.

Blum, Deborah. *Ghost Hunters: William James and the Search for Scientific Proof of Life After Death*, 2006, The Penguin Press.

Bohak, Gideon. *Ancient Jewish Magic*, 2008, Cambridge University Press.

Bolt, Peter G. *Jesus' Defeat of Death: Persuading Mark's Early Readers*, 2003, Cambridge University Press.

Bond, Helen K. *The Historical Jesus: A Guide for the Perplexed*, 2012, T&T Clark.

Bonner, Campbell. "Traces of Thaumaturgic Technique in the Miracles," *Harvard Theological Review* 20 (1927) 171-81.

Brandon, Samuel G.F. "The Historical Element in Primitive Christianity," *Numen* 2 (1955) 156-67.

Brashear, William M. "The Greek Magical Papyri: An Introduction and Survey, Annotated Bibliography (1928-1994)," *Aufstieg und Niedergang der römischen Welt* II, 18.5 3380-3730, H. Temporini & W. Haase, eds, Walter de Gruyer.

Brower, Kent. "Mark 9:1: Seeing the Kingdom in Power," *Journal for the Study of the New Testament* 6 (1980) 17-41.

Brown, Christopher. "Dionysus and the Women of Elis: PMG 871," *Greek, Roman, and Byzantine Studies* 23 (1982) 305-14.

Brown, Frank E. "Violation of Sepulture in Palestine," *The American Journal of Philology* 52 (1931) 1-29.

Bryen, Ari Z. & Andrzej Wypustek. "Gemellus' Evil Eyes (P.Mich. VI 423-424)," *Greek, Roman, and Byzantine Studies* 49 (2009) 535-55.

Burkert, Walter. "Greek Tragedy and Sacrificial Ritual," *Greek, Roman, and Byzantine Studies* 7 (1966) 87-121.

_. *Homo Necans: The Anthropology of Ancient Greek Sacrificial Ritual and Myth*, Peter Bing, tr, 1983, University of California Press.

_. *Greek Religion: Archaic and Classic*, 1985, Harvard University Press.

_. *Ancient Mystery Cults*, 1987, Harvard University Press.

_. *The Orientalizing Revolution: Near Eastern Influence on Greek Culture in the Early Archaic Age*, M.E. Pindar, tr, 1992, *Harvard University Press*.

Burkill, T.A. "The Last Supper," *Numen* 3 (1956) 161-77.

Chadwick, Henry. "Origen, Celsus, and the Resurrection of the Body," *Harvard Theological Review* 41 (1948) 82-102.

_. *Origen: Contra Celsum*, 1965, Cambridge University Press.

Cabal, Ted. "Defending the Resurrection of Jesus: Yesterday, Today and Forever," *The Southern Baptist Journal of Theology* 18 (2014) 115-37.

Carrier, Richard. "The Guarded Tomb of Jesus and Daniel in the Lion's Den: An Argument for the Plausibility of Theft," *Journal of Higher Criticism* 8 (2001) 304-18.

Chatley, Herbert. "Mediæval Occultism," *The Monist* 18 (1908) 510-16.

Cheek, John L. "The Historicity of the Markan Resurrection Narrative," *Journal of Bible and Religion* 27 (1959) 191-200.

Clarke, Isabel. "Psychosis and spirituality: the discontinuity model," *Psychosis and Spirituality: Exploring the new frontier*, I. Clarke ed, 2001, Whurr Publishers.

Clarke, Roger. *Ghosts A Natural History: 500 Years of Searching for Proof*, 2012, St. Martin's Press.

Combs, Jason Robert. "A Ghost on the Water? Understanding an Absurdity in Mark 6:49-50," *Journal of Biblical Literature* 127 (2008) 345-58.

Conner, Robert. *Jesus the Sorcerer: Exorcist and Prophet of the Apocalypse*, 2006, Mandrake of Oxford.

_. *Magic in Christianity: From Jesus to the Gnostics*, 2014, Mandrake of Oxford.

_. *The "Secret" Gospel of Mark: Morton Smith, Clement of Alexandria, and Four Decades of Academic Burlesque*, 2015, Mandrake of Oxford.

Conybeare, Frederick C. (tr). *The Life of Apollonius of Tyana* II, 1921, Harvard University Press.

Conzelmann, Hans. "On the Analysis of the Confessional Formula in 1 Corinthians 15:3-5, *Interpretation: A Journal of Bible and Theology* 20 (1966) 15-25.

Craffert, Pieter F. "Did Jesus Rise Bodily From the Dead? Yes and no!" *Religion and Theology* 15 (2008) 133-53.

_. "Jesus' Resurrection in a Social-Scientific Perspective: Is There Anything New to be Said?" *Journal for the Study of the Historical Jesus* 7 (2009) 126-51.

Crossan, John Dominic. "Bias in Interpreting Earliest Christianity," *Numen* 39 (1992) 233-35.

_. *Who Killed Jesus? Exposing the Roots of Anti-Semitism in the Gospel Story of the Death of Jesus*, 1995, Harper San Francisco.

_. "The Resurrection of Jesus in Its Jewish Context," *Neotestamentica* 37 (2003) 29-57.

Crawford, Barry S. "Near Expectation in the Sayings of Jesus," *Journal of Biblical Literature* 101 (1982) 225-44.

Daniel, Robert W. & Franco Maltomini, eds, *Supplementum Magicum*, I (1990) & II (1992), Westdeutscher Verlag.

David, Rosalie. *Religion and Magic in Ancient Egypt*, 2002, Penguin Books.

Davies, T. Witton. *Magic, Divination, and Demonology Among the Hebrews and Their Neighbors: Including an Examination of Biblical References and of the Biblical Terms*, 1898, J. Clarke & Company (reprinted, Ktav Publishing House, 1969).

Dein, Simon. "Mental Health and the Paranormal," *Journal of Transpersonal Studies* 31 (2012) 61-74.

DeMaris, Richard E. "Corinthian Religion and Baptism for the Dead (1 Corinthians 15:29): Insights from Archaeology and Anthropology," *Journal of Biblical Literature* 114 (1995) 661-82.

DeVine, Charles F. "The 'Blood of God' in Acts 20:28," *Catholic Biblical Quarterly* 9 (1947) 381-408.

Devinsky, Orrin & George Lai. "Spirituality and Religion in Epilepsy," *Epilepsy and Behavior* 12 (2008) 636-43.

Dewhurst, Kenneth & A.W. Beard. "Sudden Religious Conversions in Temporal Lobe Epilepsy," *British Journal of Psychiatry* 117 (1970) 497-507.

Dolansky, Fanny. "Mourning the Family Dead on the Parentalia: Ceremony, Spectacle, and Memory," *Phoenix* 65 (2011) 125-57.

Ehrhardt, Arnold. "The Disciples of Emmaus," *New Testament Studies* (1964) 182-201.

Ehrman, Bart D. *The New Testament: A Historical Introduction to the Early Christian Writings*, 3rd ed, 2004, Oxford University Press.

Eitrem, Samson. *Some Notes on the Demonology in the New Testament*, 2nd edition revised and enlarged, 1966, Symbolae Osloenses, Supplement XX.

_. "Dreams and Divination in Magic Ritual," *Magika Hiera: Ancient Greek Magic and Religion*, C. Faraone & D. Obbink, eds, 1991, Oxford University Press.

Eller, David. "A Mind Is a Terrible Thing: How Evolved Cognitive Biases Lead to Religion (and Other Mental Errors), *Christianity in the Light of Science: Critically Examining the World's Largest Religion*, J.W. Loftus, ed, 2016, Prometheus Books.

Epp, Eldon Jay. "The Multivalence of the Term 'Original Text' in New Testament Textual Criticism," *Harvard Theological Review* 92 (1999) 245-281.

_. "The Disputed Words of the Eucharistic Institution (Luke 22:19b-20): The Long and Short of the Matter," *Biblica* 90 (2009) 407-16.

Erlendur, Haraldsson. "Survey of Claimed Encounters with the Dead," *Omega: Journal of Death and Dying* 19 (1988-89) 103-13.

Evans, Hilary & Patrick Huyghe. *The Field Guide to Ghosts and Other Apparitions*, 2000, Quill.

Faierstein, Morris M. "Why Do the Scribes Say That Elijah Must Come First," *Journal of Biblical Literature* 100 (1981) 75-86.

Fairbanks, Arthur. "The Chthonic Gods of Greek Religion," *The American Journal of Philology* 21 (1900) 241-59.

Faraone, Christopher A. "Aeschylus' [*humnos desmios*] (Eum. 306) and Attic Judicial Curse Tablets," *Journal of Hellenic Studies* 105 (1985) 150-54.

Felton, Debbie. *Haunted Greece and Rome: Ghost Stories from Classical Antiquity*, 1999, University of Texas Press.

Ferguson, Everette. *Backgrounds of Early Christianity*, 3rd ed, 2003, William B. Eerdmans Publishing Company.

Finucane, Ronald C. *Ghosts: Appearances of the Dead and Cultural Transformation*, 1996, Prometheus Books.

Fisher, Edmund W. "'Let Us look upon the Blood-of-Christ,' (1 Clement 7:4)," *Vigiliae Christianae* 34 (1980) 218-36.

Francis, James A. "Truthful Fiction: New Questions to Old Answers on Philostratus' 'Life of Apollonius,'" *American Journal of Philology* 119 (1998) 419-41.

Frankfurter, David. "Fetus Magic and Sorcery Fears in Roman Egypt," *Greek, Roman, and Byzantine Studies* 46 (2006) 37-62.

_. "Where the Spirits Dwell: Possession, Christianization, and Saints' Shrines in Late Antiquity," *Harvard Theological Review* 103 (2010) 27-46.

Frayer-Griggs, Daniel. "'More Than a Prophet': Echoes of Exorcism in Markan and Matthean Baptist Traditions," *Matthew and Mark Across Perspectives: Essays in Honour of Stephen C. Barton and William R. Telford*, K.A. Bendorais & N.K. Gupta, eds, 2016, T&T Clark.

Fuhrmann, Christopher J. *Policing the Roman Empire: Soldiers, Administration and Public Order*, 2012, Oxford University Press.

Gager, John G. *Kingdom and Community: The Social World of Early Christianity*, 1975, Prentice Hall.

Gagné, Renaud. "Winds and Ancestors: The 'Physika' of Orpheus," *Harvard Studies in Classical Philology* 103 (2007) 1-23.

Garrett, Susan R. *The Demise of the Devil: Magic and the Demonic in Luke's Writings*, 1989, Fortress Press.

Giannobile, Segio & D.R. Jordan. "A Lead Phylactery from Colle san Basilio (Sicily)," *Greek, Roman, and Byzantine Studies* 46 (2006) 73-86.

Gilmour, Samuel MacLean. "The Christophany to More Than Five Hundred Brethern," *Journal of Biblical Literature* 80 (1961) 248-52.

Goldin, Judah. "The Magic of Magic and Superstition," *Aspects of Religious Propaganda in Judaism and Christianity*, 1976, E. Schüssler Fiorenza, ed, University of Notre Dame Press.

Gordon, Richard. "Imagining Greek and Roman Magic," *Witchcraft and Magic in Europe: Ancient Greece and Rome*, B. Ankarloo & S. Clark, eds, 1999, University of Pennsylvania Press.

Goulder, Michael. "Jesus' Resurrection and Christian Origins: A Re-sponse to N.T. Wright," *Journal for the Study of the Historical Jesus* 3 (2005) 187-95.

Grant, Robert M. "The Resurrection of the Body," *The Journal of Religion* 28 (1948) 120-30, 188-208.

Greyson, Bruce & Mitchell B. Liester. "Auditory Hallucinations Following Near-Death Experiences," *Journal of Humanistic Psychology* 44 (2004) 320-36.

Grig, Lucy. *Making Martyrs in Late Antiquity*, 2004, Duckworth.

Gurney, Edmund, Myers, Frederic W.H. & Podmore, Frank. *Phantasms of the Living*, Vol. I, 1886, Trübner & Company.

Hamori, Esther J. "The Prophet and the Necromancer: Women's Divination for Kings," *Journal of Biblical Literature* 132 (2013) 827-43.

Hanse, Hermann. "[echo]," *Theological Dictionary of the New Testament*, G. Kittel, ed, 1964, William B. Eerdmans.

Hansen, William. *Phlegon of Tralles' Book of Marvels*, 1996, University of Exeter Press.

Haraldsson, Erlendur. "Survey of Claimed Encounters With the Dead," *Omega–Journal of Death and Dying* 19 (1988-89) 103-13.

_ & Joop M. Houtkooper. "Traditional Christian Beliefs, Spiritualism, and the Paranormal: An Icelandic-American Comparison," *The International Journal for the Psychology of Religion* 6 (1996) 51-64.

Harmon, Austin M. (tr), *Lucian*, III, 1921, Harvard University Press.

Harrison, Jane E. "Delphika. (A) The Erinyes. (B). The Omphalos," *Journal of Hellenic Studies* 19 (1899) 205-51.

Harrison, James R. "In Quest of the Third Heaven: Paul and His Apocalyptic Imitators," *Vigiliae Christianae* 58 (2004) 24-55.

Hartog, Paul. "Greco-Roman Understanding of Christianity," *The Routledge Companion to Early Christian Thought*, D.J. Bingham, ed, 2010, Routledge.

Hatch, William H.P., "The Use of [*alitērios, araios, enagēs, enthumios*], and [*prostropaios*]: A Study in Greek Lexicography," *Harvard Studies in Classical Philology* 19 (1908) 157-86.

Hauck, Robert J. "'They Saw What They Said They Saw;: Sense Knowledge in Early Christian Polemic," *Harvard Theological Review* 81 (1988) 239-49.

Headlam, Walter. "Ghost-Raising, Magic, and the Underworld," *The Classical Review* 16 (1902) 52-61.

Heard, Kenneth V. & Stuart A. Vyse. "Authoritarianism and Paranormal Beliefs," *Imagination, Cognition, and Personality* 18 (1998-99) 121-26.

Herman, Gabriel. "Greek Epiphanies and the Sensed Presence," *Historia: Zeitschrift für Alte Geschichte* 60 (2011) 127-57.

Herrero de Jáuregui, Miguel. *Orphism and Christianity in Late Antiquity*, 2010, De Gruyter.

Hoehner, Harold W. *Herod Antipas: A Contemporary of Jesus Christ*, 1972, Cambridge University Press.

Horsley, Richard A. "'How Can Some of You Say There Is No Resurrection of the Dead?' Spiritual Elitism in Corinth," *Novum Testamen-tum* 20 (1978) 203-31.

Houston, Susan H. "Ghost Riders in the Sky," *Western Folklore* 23 (1964) 153-62.

Howe, E. Margaret. "... But Some Doubted." (Matt. 28:17) A Reappraisal of Factors Influencing the Easter Faith of the Early Christian Community," *Journal of the Evangelical Theological Society* 18 (1975) 173-80.

Hull, John M. *Hellenistic Magic and the Synoptic Tradition*, 1974, SCM Press Ltd.

Irwin, Harvey J. "Belief in the Paranormal: A Review of the Empirical Literature," *Journal of the American Society for Psychical Research* 87 (1993) 1-39.

_. Neil Dagnall & Kenneth Drinkwater. "Paranormal Beliefs and Cognitive Processes Underlying the Formation of Delusions," *Australian Journal of Parapsychology* 12 (2012) 107-26.

Jackson, Mike. "Psychotic and spiritual experience: a case study comparison," *Psychosis and Spirituality: Exploring the new frontier*, I. Clarke, ed, 2001, Whurr Publishers.

Jacoby, Felix. "[*GENESIA*]: A Forgotten Festival of the Dead," *The Classical Quarterly* 38 (1944) 67-71.

James, E.O. "The Influence of Folklore on the History of Religion," *Numen* 9 (1962) 1-16.

Janowitz, Naomi. "Theories of Divine Names in Origen and Pseudo-Dionysius," *History of Religions* 30 (1991) 359-72.

_. *Icons of Power: Ritual Practices in Late Antiquity*, 2002, Pennsylvania State University Press.

Jeffers, Ann. *Magic and Divination in Ancient Palestine and Syria*, 1996, E.J. Brill.

Jennings, Theodore W., Jr. & Tat-Siong Benny Liew. "Mistaken Identities But Model Faith: Rereading the Centurion, the Chap, and the Christ in Matthew 8:5-13," *Journal of Biblical Literature* 123 (2004) 467-94.

Johnston, Sarah Iles. *Restless Dead: Encounters between the Living and the Dead in Ancient Greece*, 1999, University of California Press.

Jones, Christopher P. *Culture and Society in Lucian*, 1986, Harvard University Press.

Jordan, David R. "P. Duke.inv.230, an Erotic Spell," *Greek, Roman, and Byzantine Studies* 40 (1999) 159-70.

Kannaday, Wayne C. *Apologetic Discourse and the Scribal Tradition: Evidence of the Influence of Apologetic Interests on the Text of the Canonical Gospels*, 2004, Society of Biblical Literature.

_. "'Are Your *Intentions* Honorable?': Apologetic Interests and Scribal Revision of Jesus in the Canonical Gospels," *TC: A Journal of Biblical Textual Criticism* 11 (2006) online.

Karagulla, Shafica. "Psychical Phenomena in Temporal Lobe Epilepsy and the Psychoses," *British Medical Journal* (March 26, 1955) 748-52.

Kearney, Peter J. "He Appeared To 500 Brothers (1 COR. XV 6)," *Novum Testamentum* 22 (1980) 264-84.

Kelhoffer, James A. "The Apostle Paul and Justin Martyr on the Miraculous: A Comparison of Appeals to Authority," *Greek, Roman, and Byzantine Studies* 42 (2001) 163-84.

Kelley, Michael P. "Corellates of Paranormal Beliefs, I: Schizotypy," *The Journal of Parapsychology* 75 (2011) 301-25.

Kennard, J. Spencer. "The Burial of Jesus," *Journal of Biblical Literature* 74 (1955) 227-38.

Kennedy, J.E. "Personality and Motivation to Believe, Misbelieve, and Disbelieve in Paranormal Phenomena," *Journal of Parapsychology* 69 (2005) 263-92.

Kent, Stephen A. "Narcissistic Fraud in the Ancient World: Lucian's Account of Alexander of Abonuteichos and the Cult of Glycon," *Ancient Narrative* 6 (2007) 77-99.

Kirby, Peter. "The Case Against the Empty Tomb," *Journal of Higher Criticism* 9 (2002) 175-202.

_. "The Case Against the Empty Tomb," *The Empty Tomb: Jesus Beyond the Grave*, R.M. Price & J.J. Lowder, eds, 2005, Prometheus Books.

Kittredge, George Lyman. "Arm-Pitting among the Greeks," *The American Journal of Philology* 6 (1885) 151-69.

Kodell, Jerome. *The Eucharist in the New Testament*, 1988, The Liturgical Press.

Kotansky, Roy. "Incantations and Prayers for Salvation on Inscribed Greek Amulets," *Magika Hiera: Ancient Greek Magic and Religion*, C. Faraone & D. Obbink, eds, 1991, Oxford University Press.

_. *Greek Magical Amulets: The Inscribed Gold, Silver, Copper, and Bronze Lamellae, Part I, Published Texts of Known Provenance*, 1994, Westdeutscher Verlag.

Kraeling, Carl H. "Was Jesus Accused of Necromancy?" *Journal of Biblical Literature* 59 (1940) 147-57.

Kraemer, Ross S. "Implicating Herodias and Her Daughter in the Death of John the Baptizer: A (Christian) Theological Strategy?" *Journal of Biblical Literature* 125 (2006) 321-49.

Kreitzer, Larry J. "The Plutonium of Hierapolis and the Descent of Christ into 'the Lowermost Parts of the Earth,'" *Biblica* 79 (1998) 381-93.

Kroeger, Catherine. "The Apostle Paul and the Greco-Roman Cults of Women," *Journal of the Evangelical Theological Society* 30 (1987) 25-38.

Lalleman, Pieter J. "Polymorphy of Christ," *The Apocryphal Acts of John*, J.N. Bremmer, ed, 1995, Pharos.

Landsborough, D. "St Paul and temporal lobe epilepsy," *Journal of Neurology, Neurosurgery, and Psychiatry* 50 (1987) 659-64.

Larøi, Frank, et alia. "Culture and Hallucinations: Overview and Future Directions," *Schizophrenia Bulletin* 40 (2014) S213-S220.

Lecouteaux, Claude. *The Return of the Dead: Ghosts, Ancestors, and the Transparent Veil of the Pagan Mind*, J.E. Graham (tr), 1996, Inner Traditions.

LiDonnici, Lynn. "Burning for It: Erotic Spells for Fever and Compulsion in the Ancient Mediterranean World," *Greek, Roman, and Byzantine Studies* 39 (1998) 63-98.

Leipoldt, Johannes. "The Resurrection Stories," *Journal of Higher Criticism* 4 (1997) 138-49.

Lincoln, Andrew T. "The Promise and the Failure: Mark 16:7, 8," *Journal of Biblical Literature* 108 (1989) 283-300.

Lindars, Barnabas. "The Sound of the Trumpet: Paul and Eschatology," *Bulletin of the John Rylands Library* 67 (1984-85) 766-82.

Lindeman, Marjaana & Annika M. Svedholm. "What's in a Term? Paranormal, Superstitious, Magical and Supernatural Beliefs by Any Other Name Would Mean the Same," *Review of General Psychology* 16 (2012) 241-55.

Louw, Johannes P. & Eugene A. Nida, eds, *Greek-English Lexicon of the New Testament Based on Semantic Domains*, 2nd ed, 1988, United Bible Societies.

Lowder, Jeffery Jay. "Historical Evidence and the Empty Tomb Story: A Reply to William Lane Craig," *Journal of Higher Criticism* 8 (2001) 251-93.

Luck, Georg. "Witches and Sorcerers in Classical Literature," *Witchcraft and Magic in Europe: Ancient Greece and Rome*, B. Ankarloo & S. Clark, eds, 1999, University of Pennsylvania Press.

Maccoby, Hyam. *The Mythmaker: Paul and the Invention of Christianity*, 1986, Harper Collins.

MacDonald, Margaret Y. *Early Christian Women and Pagan Opinion: The Power of the Hysterical Woman*, 1996, Cambridge University Press.

Maclaurin, E.C.B. "Beelzeboul," *Novum Testamentum* 20.2 (1978) 156-60.

Magoulias, Harry J. "The Lives of Byzantine Saints as Sources of Data for the History of Magic in the Sixth and Seventh Centuries A.D.: Sorcery, Relics and Icons," *Byzantion* 37 (1967) 228-69.

Mánek, Jindrich. "The Apostle Paul and the Empty Tomb," *Novum Testamentum* 2 (1958) 276-80.

Marcovich, Miroslav. *Origenes: Contra Celsum Libri VIII*, 2001, Brill Academic Publishers.

Margolioth, Mordecai. *Sepher Ha-Razim*, 1966, Yediot Achronot.

Marshall, Ian H. "The Resurrection of Jesus in Luke," *Tyndale Bulletin* 24 (1973) 55-98.

Martin, James P. "History and Eschatology in the Lazarus Narrative: John 11:1-44," *Scottish Journal of Theology* 17 (1964) 332-43.

Mastrocinque, Attilio. "Late Antique Lamps with Defixiones," *Greek, Roman, and Byzantine Studies* 47 (2007) 87-99.

Maurizio, Lisa. "Anthropology and Spirit Possession: A Reconsideration of the Pythia's Role at Delphi," *Journal of Hellenic Studies* 115 (1995) 69-86.

Menezes Jr., Adair & Alexander Moreira-Almeida. "Religion, Spirituality, and Psychosis," *Current Psychiatry Reports* 12 (2010) 174-79.

Meyer, Marvin & Richard Smith. *Ancient Christian Magic: Coptic Texts of Ritual Power*, 1994, Harper San Francisco.

Miller, Richard C. "Mark's Empty Tomb and Other Translation Fables in Classical Antiquity," *Journal of Biblical Literature* 129 (2010) 759-76.

Miller, Robert J. "When It's Futile to Argue about Historical Jesus: A Response to Bock, Keener, and Webb," *Journal for the Study of the Historical Jesus* 9 (2011) 85-95.

Mitchell, Matthew W. "Bodiless Demons and Written Gospels: Reflections on 'The Gospel According to the Hebrews' in the Apostolic Fathers," *Novum Testamentum* 52 (2010) 221-40.

Montanari, Franco. *The Brill Dictionary of Ancient Greek*, 2015, Brill.

Morgan, Michael A. *Sepher Ha-Razim: The Book of the Mysteries*, H.W. Attridge, ed, 1983, Scholars Press.

Mount, Christopher. "1 Corinthians 11:3-16: Spirit Possession and Authority in a Non-Pauline Interpolation," *Journal of Biblical Literature* 124 (2005) 313-40.

Murphy-O'Connor, Jerome. "Tradition and Redaction in 1 Cor 15:3-7," *Catholic Biblical Quarterly* 43 (1981) 582-89.

Myllykoski, Matti. "Being There: The Function of the Supernatural in Acts 1-12," *Wonders Never Cease: The Purpose of Narrative Miracle Stories in the New Testament and its Religious Environment*, M. Labahn & B.J.L. Peerbolte, eds, 2006, T&T Clark.

Naveh, Joseph & Shaul Shaked. *Magic Spells and Formulae: Aramaic Incantations of Late Antiquity*, 1993, Magnes Press.

Nock, A.D. "Tertullian and the Ahori," *Vigiliae Christianae* 4 (1950) 129-41.

Nodet, Étienne. "On Jesus' Last Supper," *Biblica* 91 (2010) 348-69.

_. "On Jesus' last week(s)," *Biblica* 92 (2011) 204-30.

O'Connell, Jake. "Did Greco-Roman Apparitional Models Influence Luke's Resurrection Narrative? A Response to Deborah Thompson Prince," *Journal of Greco-Roman Christianity and Judaism* 5 (2008) 190-99.

Ogden, Daniel. *Greek and Roman Necromancy*, 2001, Princeton University Press.

_. "The Ancient Greek Oracles of the Dead," *Acta Classica* 44 (2001) 167-95.

_. *In Search of the Sorcerer's Apprentice: The traditional tales of Lucian's Lover of Lies*, 2007, The Classical Press of Wales.

_. *Magic, Witchcraft, and Ghosts in the Greek and Roman Worlds: A Sourcebook*, 2nd ed, 2009, Oxford University Press.

Ogle, Marbury B. "The House-Door in Greek and Roman Religion and Folk Lore," *The American Journal of Philology* 32 (1911) 251-71.

Osbourne, Grant R. "Historical Criticism and the Evangelical," *Journal of the Evangelical Theological Society* 42 (1999) 193-210.

Pachoumi, Eleni. "Resurrection of the Body in the *Greek Magical Papyri*," *Numen* 58 (2011) 729-740.

_. "The Erotic and Separation Spells of the Magical Papyri and *Defixiones*," *Greek, Roman, and Byzantine Studies* 53 (2013) 294-325.

Parker, Simon B. "Possession Trance and Prophecy in Pre-Exile Israel," *Vetus Testamentum* 28 (1978) 271-85.

Pearson, Birger A. "1 Thessalonians 2:13-16: A Deutero-Pauling Interpolation," *Harvard Theological Review* 64 (1971) 79-94.

Pease, Arthur Stanley. "Some Aspects of Invisibility," *Harvard Studies in Classical Philology* 53 (1942) 1-36.

Persinger, Michael. "Religious and Mystical Experiences as Artifacts of Temporal Lobe Function: A General Hypothesis," *Perceptual and Motor Skills* 57 (1983) 1255-62.

Peters, Emmanuelle, et alia. "Delusional ideation in religious and psychotic populations," *British Journal of Clinical Psychology* 38 (1999) 83-96.

_. "Are Delusions on a Continuum? The case of religious and delusional beliefs," *Psychosis and Spirituality: Exploring the new frontier*, I. Clarke, ed, 2001, Whurr Publishers Ltd.

Petropoulou, Angeliki. "The Interment of Patroklos (Iliad 23.252-57)," *The American Journal of Philology* 109 (1988) 482, 495.

Philostratus, Flavius. *The Life of Apollonius of Tyana*, I & II, F.C. Conybeare (tr), 1912, Harvard University Press.

Pickup, Martin. "'On the Third Day': The Time Frame of Jesus' Death and Resurrection," *Journal of the Evangelical Theological Society* 56 (2013) 511-42.

Pinch, Geraldine. *Magic in Ancient Egypt*, 1994, University of Texas Press.

Powell, Mark Allan. "Evangelical Christians and Historical-Jesus Studies: Final Reflections," *Journal for the Study of the Historical Jesus* 9 (2011) 124-36.

Preisendanz, Karl. *Papyri Graecae Magicae: Die Grieschischen Zauberpapyri*, I & II, 2001, K.G. Saur.

Price, Robert M. "Apocryphal Apparitions: 1 Corinthians 15:3-11 as a Post-Pauline Interpolation," *The Empty Tomb: Jesus Beyond the Grave*, R.M. Price & J.J. Lowder, eds, 2005, Prometheus Books.

Prince, Deborah Thompson. "The 'Ghost' of Jesus: Luke 24 in Light of Ancient Narratives of Post-Mortem Apparition," *Journal for the Study of the New Testament* 29 (2007) 287-301.

___. "'Why Do You Seek the Living among the Dead?' Rhetorical Questions in the Lukan Resurrection Narrative," *Journal of Biblical Literature* 135 (2016) 123-39.

Quarles, Charles. "[*META THN EGERSIN AUTOU*]: A Scribal Interpolation in Matthew 27:53?" *Journal of the Evangelical Theological Society* 59 (2016) 271-86.

Rabinowitz, Jacob. *The Rotting Goddess: The Origin of the Witch in Classical Antiquity's Demonization of Fertility Religion*, 1998, Automedia.

Reimer, Andy M. *Miracle and Magic: A Study in the Acts of the Apostles and the Life of Apollonius of Tyana*, 2002, JSNT Supplement Series 235.

Renehan, Robert. "On the Greek Origins of the Concepts Incorporeality and Immateriality," *Greek, Roman, and Byzantine Studies* 21 (1980) 105-38.

Rice, David G. & John E. Stambaugh. *Sources for the Study of Greek Religion*, corrected edition, 2009, The Society of Biblical Literature.

Ricks, Steven D. "The Magician as Outsider in the Hebrew Bible and the New Testament," *Ancient Magic and Ritual Power*, M. Meyer & P. Mirecki, eds, 2001, Brill Academic Publishers.

Riess, Ernst. "Superstitions and Popular Beliefs in Greek Comedy," *American Journal of Philology* 18 (1897) 189-205.

Riley, Gregory J. *Resurrection Reconsidered: Thomas and John in Controversy*, 1995, Fortress Press.

Ritner, Robert K. "Necromancy in Ancient Egypt," *Magic and Divination in the Ancient World*, L. Ciraolo & J. Seidel, eds, 2002, Brill.

Roberts, Alexander & James Donaldson, eds. *Ante-Nicene Christian Library: Translations of the Writings of the Fathers Down to A.D. 325*, T&T Clark, 1870.

Robinson, James M. "Jesus from Easter to Valentinus (Or to the Apostles' Creed)," *Journal of Biblical Literature* 101 (1982) 5-37.

Rock, Adam J. et alia. "The Effect of Shamanic-like Stimulus Conditions and the Cognitive-perceptual Factor of Schizotypy on Phenomenology," *North American Journal of Psychology* 10 (2008) 79-98.

Rose, H.J. "Ghost Ritual in Aeschylus," *Harvard Theological Review* 43 (1950) 257-80.

Royalty, Jr, Robert M. "Dwelling on Visions. On the Nature of the so-called 'Colossians Heresy,'" *Biblica* 83 (2002) 329-57.

Rudhardt, Jean. "Sur la possibilité de comprendre une religion antique," *Numen* 11 (1964) 189-211.

Samain, P. "L'accusation de magie contre le Christ dans les évangiles," *Ephemerides Theologicae Lovanienses* 15 (1932) 449-90.

Schäfer, Peter. *Jesus in the Talmud*, 2007, Princeton University Press.

Schmidt, Brian B. *Israel's Beneficent Dead: Ancestor Cult and Necromancy in Ancient Israelite Religion and Tradition*, 1996, Eisenbrauns.

Schmidt, Daryl. "1 Thess 2:13-16: Linguistic Evidence for an Interpolation," *Journal of Biblical Literature* 102 (1983) 269-79.

Schürer, Emil. *A History of the Jewish People in the Time of Jesus Christ*, 1941, Schoken Publishing House.

Scott, William. "Gospels in a Developing Church," *Journal of Bible and Religion* 12 (1944) 19-25.

Scroggs, Robin & Kent I. Groff. "Baptism in Mark: Dying and Rising with Christ," *Journal of Biblical Literature* 92 (1973) 531-48.

Seaford, Richard. *Dionysos*, 2006, Routledge.

Šedina, Miroslav. "Magical Power of Names in Origen's Polemic Against Celsus," *Listy filologické* 136 (2013) 7-25.

Setzer, Claudia. "Excellent Women: Female Witnesses to the Resurrection," *Journal of Biblical Literature* 116 (1997) 259-72.

Shannon, Kelly E. "Authenticating the Marvelous: *Mirabilia* in Pliny the Younger, Tacitus, and Suetonius," *Working Papers on Nervan, Trajanic and Hadrianic Literature* 1.9 (2013).

Sider, Ronald J. "St. Paul's Understanding of the Nature and Significance of the Resurrection in 1 Corinthians XV 1-19," *Novum Testamentum* 19 (1977) 124-41.

Smelik, Klaas A.D. "The Witch of Endor: 1 Samuel 28 in Rabbinic and Christian Exegesis Till 800 A.D.," *Vigiliae Christianae* 33 (1977) 160-79.

Smith, Daniel A. "Revisiting the Empty Tomb: The Post-Mortem Vindication of Jesus in Mark and Q," *Novum Testamentum* 45 (2003) 123-37.

_. "Seeing a Pneuma(tic Body): The Apologetic Interests of Luke 24:36-43," *Catholic Biblical Quarterly* 72 (2010) 752-72.

Smith, Morton. *Jesus the Magician: Charlatan or Son of God?* 1978, Harper & Row.

_. *Studies in the Cult of Yahweh*, II, S.J.D. Cohen, ed, 1996, E.J. Brill.

Smith, Preserved. "Christian Theophagy: An Historical Sketch," *The Monist* 28/2 (1918) 161-208.

Smith, Robert H. "The Tomb of Jesus," *The Biblical Archaeologist* 30 (1967) 74-90.

Smith, Wesley D. "So-Called Possession in Pre-Christian Greece," *Transactions and Proceedings of the American Philological Association* 96 (1965) 403-26.

Snape, H.C. "After the Crucifixion or 'The Great Forty Days,'" *Numen* 17 (1970) 188-99.

Spilka, Bernard, Phillip Shaver & Lee A. Kirkpatrick. "A General Attribution Theory for the Psychology of Religion," *Journal for the Scientific Study of Religion* 24 (1985) 1-20.

Spoer, Hans H. "Notes on Jewish Amulets," *Journal of Biblical Literature* 23.2 (1904) 97-105.

Stein, Robert H. "Is the Transfiguration (Mark 9:2-8) a Misplaced Resurrection-Account?" *Journal of Biblical Literature* 95 (1976) 79-96.

_. "Is Our Reading the Bible the Same as the Original Audience's Hearing It? A Case Study in the Gospel of Mark," *Journal of the Evangelical Theological Society* 46 (2003) 63-78.

Strelan, Rick. *Strange Acts: Studies in the Cultural World of the Acts of the Apostles*, 2004, Walter de Gruyter.

Tabor, James D. "'Returning to the Divinity': Josephus's Portrayal of the Disappearances of Enoch, Elijah, and Moses," *Journal of Biblical Literature* 108 (1989) 225-38.

Thalbourne, Michael A., Susan E. Crawley & James Houran. "Temporal lobe lability in the highly transliminal mind," *Personality and Individual Differences* 35 (2003) 1965-74.

Thaniel, George. "Lemures and Larvae," *The American Journal of Philology* 94 (1973) 182-87.

Thee, Francis C.R. *Julius Africanus and the Early Christian View of Magic*, 1984, Mohr Siebeck.

Tierney, Michael. "A New Ritual of the Orphic Mysteries," *The Classical Quarterly* 16/2 (1922) 77-87.

Trimble, Michael & Anthony Freeman. "An investigation of religiosity and the Gastaut-Geschwind syndrome in patients with temporal lobe epilepsy," *Epilepsy and Behavior* 9 (2006) 407-14.

Tropper, Joseph. "Spirit of the Dead [ōb]," *Dictionary of Deities and Demons in the Bible*, K. van der Toorn, B. Becking & P.W. van der Horst, eds, 1995, E.J. Brill.

Turner, Eric G. "The *Phasma* of Menander," *Greek, Roman, and Byzantine Studies* 10 (1969) 307-324.

Vaitl, Dieter, et. alia. "Psychobiology of Altered States of Consciousness," *Psychological Bulletin* 131 (2005) 98-127.

Vermeule, Emily. *Aspects of Death in Early Greek Art and Poetry*, 1979, University of California Press.

Vincent, Ken R. "Resurrection Appearances of Jesus as After-Death Communication," *Journal of Near-Death Studies* 30 (2012) 137-148.

_. "Resurrection Appearances of Jesus as After-Death Communication: Rejoinder to Gary Habermas," *Journal of Near-Death Studies* 30 (2012) 159-66.

Walker, William O. "Postcrucifixion Appearances and Christian Origins," *Journal of Biblical Literature* 88 (1969) 157-65.

_. "Text-Critical Evidence for Interpolations in the Letters of Paul," *Catholic Biblical Quarterly* 50 (1988) 622-31.

Walsh, Roger. "What is a Shaman? Definition, Origin and Distribution," *Journal of Transpersonal Psychology* 21 (1989) 1-11.

Wedderburn, A.J.M. "The Problem of the Denial of the Resurrection in 1 Corinthians XV," *Novum Testamentum* 23 (1981) 229-41.

Weltin, Edward G. "The Concept of *Ex-Opere-Operato* Efficacy in the Fathers as an Evidence of Magic in Christianity," *Greek, Roman, and* *Byzantine Studies* 3 (1960) 74-100.

Wenham, David. "The Resurrection Narratives in Matthew's Gospel," *Tyndale Bulletin* 24 (1973) 21-54.

Wernik, Uri. "Frustrated Beliefs and Early Christianity: A Psychological Enquiry in the Gospels of the New Testament," *Numen* 22 (1975) 96-130.

Winkler, Jack. "Lollianos and the Desperados," *The Journal of Hellenic Studies* 100 (1980) 155-81.

Wortley, John. "Some Light on Magic and Magicians in Late Antiquity," *Greek, Roman, and Byzantine Studies* 42 (2001) 289-307.

Wright, G.R.H. "Joseph's Grave Under the Tree by the Omphalos at Shechem," *Vetus Testamentum* 22 (1972) 476-86.

Wypustek, Andrzej. "Magic, Montanism, Perpetua, and the Severan Persecution," *Vigiliae Christianae* 51 (1997) 276-97.

Index

after-death communication, 60.
Angles of Mons, 126.
Anthesteria, 17, 27.
Apollonius of Tyana, 37, 121, 123.
auditory driving, 62.

Bacchae, 54-55.
battle apparitions, 126.
blindness (following seizure), 66.
bothros, 18, 104.
burial, 21, 53-54, 74, 90-92, 104.

Celsus
 Christianity as magic, 96, 146.
 resurrection as ghost story, 4, 96, 129, 155.
 witness reliability, 127-128.
 women unreliable witnesses, 96, 118, 127.

Christophany, 83.
cognitive closure, 67.
confirmation bias, 67-68.
corpse
 exposure of, 53-54.
 mutilation (see *maschalismos*, *ghosts*)
culturally determined reality, 61, 72, 98, 117, 124-25, 152-54.

demons
 know who Jesus is, 41.
Dionysus, 17, 55.
Doubting Thomas, 99, 113.

ecstasy, 56, 57, 59, 63-64, 68, 76.
empty tomb, 75, 79, 80, 85-95, 117.
energēo (perform, operate), 44, 47, 49-50.

epilepsy, 60, 65-66.
epiphany, 54, 55, 70, 127.
eschatology, 57-58, 77, 94-95, 131, 137-39, 147.
Eucharist, 78, 86-87, 139-41.
  proxy for parousia, 139.
  magic, 140-42.
  medicine of immortality, 143.

folklore, 7-8, 101-103, 154-55.

Gastaut-Geschwind syndrome, 59-60.

ghosts
  agamos (unmarried) 13, 19, 144.
  agunaios (wifeless), 13, 125, 144.
  aōros (untimely), 13, 19-20, 22, 40, 49, 144.
  apaidēs (childless), 13, 19, 125, 144.
  ataphos (unburied), 13, 19-20, 45, 74, 125.
  belief in, 3, 10, 12, 17-19, 53, 59-60, 107.
  biaiothanatos (violently killed), 13, 17, 19, 21, 39-40, 42, 45, 50, 109, 125, 126, 140.
  classes of, 12, 13-15, 40, 46, 115-16.
  conjuring of, 6, 19, 21-24, 26.
  crossroads, 111.
  daimōn (spirit), 13, 109-110.
  disease caused by, 3, 18-19, 41, 60.
  disregarded by scholars, 5-7.
  "does not have flesh and bones," 109-10.
  doors, 110-113.
  eating as proof of life, 104, 108, 116, 117, 125.
  homicides, 14, 15, 17, 19, 41.
  know the future, 41.
  lemurs (ghosts), 14, 17.
  magic, 18, 22-23, 38-41, 45, 47, 92, 111.
  mutilation of corpse, 42-43.
  necromancy, 17, 19, 45, 47, 109.

nekudaimōn (spirit of the dead) 14, 19, 21.
night (appearances), 110-111.
ōb (ghost), 14, 24-25.
phantasma (phantom), 15.
phasma (ghost), 4, 15.
pneuma (spirit), 109. 122.
possession by, 3, 18-19, 41.
pre-mortem wounds, 114-115, 125, 134.
restless ghosts, 18-21, 40-41, 49.
rituals of appeasement, 17-21.
Samuel's, 23, 24, 54.
seeing ghosts, 60, 101, 112.
sexual arousal, 64, 101, 116-18.
sudden disappearance of, 107-108.
"suppers" for, 14, 104.
tactile manifestation, 106-107, 125.
terms for, 10, 11, 13-15, 24, 40.

gospels
 composition of, 7-9, 55, 85, 87-89, 91, 93, 102-103, 110, 116, 117, 120-21, 153-55.
 contradictions in, 86, 94-95, 98, 99-100, 103, 129, 131.
 editing of, 44-45, 78-79, 85-86, 89, 92, 98, 122.
 historical value of, 7, 78, 90-91, 99-100.
 narrative shifts, 99-108.
 sources, 9, 91.

Gospel According to the Hebrews, 110.
Gospel of Peter, 121.

hallucinations, 60, 62, 65, 66, 72.
Herod the Great, 32-34, 42-43, 44, 47-48.
historiolae, 146.

incubation, 25.
insanity, 58-59, 60, 63-64, 66-68, 129.

interpolation, 75-80, 100.

Jesus (see also *ghost, resurrection, empty tomb, necromancy*)
  appears to 500 witnesses, 75-77, 83.
  authority, 31-34, 35, 37, 47.
  becomes invisible, 105.
  body not real, 89.
  burial, 73-74, 90-92, 125.
  condemned by Sanhedrin, 74.
"crucified trickster," 46.
crucifixion, 40-41, 73, 77, 78, 86-89, 92, 105, 116, 145.
  disappears at will, 123.
  embalmed, 74, 90.
  exorcist, 3, 31-36, 45-46, 145-146.
  foretells resurrection, 95.
  "ghost" of, 107, 109-118, 129.
  "has Beelzeboul," 36-38, 49.
  magician, 38-39, 42, 45-47.
  name, 34, 44, 145-147.
  necromancy, 41-48.
  not John the Baptist raised, 36, 42, 44, 47-48.
  polymorphy of, 99, 101, 123-124.
  resurrection, 68, 79-80, 88-89, 92-93, 94, 106, 110.
  sudden appearances, 110, 114.
  visions of, 54, 61, 95.

John the Baptist, 31-48.
  beheaded, 42-43.
  ghost, 43, 48, 116.
  "raised," 41-43, 44, 48.

Joseph of Arimathea, 73-74, 90.

Kraeling, Carl, 32, 37, 40, 43, 44, 47-48.

Lemuria, 17-18.
limbic system, 64.
Lucian of Samosata, 37, 45-46, 143.
  religious fraud, 128.

magic, 22-23, 38-39, 46-47, 59, 62-63, 92, 107, 118, 127, 134, 144-47.
magical papyri, 19, 21, 26, 28, 38, 40, 47, 107, 109, 117, 140, 143, 144, 146.
Martyrdom of Saint Polycarp, 25-26.
Mary Magdalene, 90, 93, 118.
maschalismos (arm-pitting) 42-43.
mediums, 6, 22, 24, 54, 58, 98.
microseizures, 61, 64.
Montanus (New Prophecy), 58-59.
music, 62-63, 64.
mysticism, 53, 60, 64-65.

near-death experiences (NDEs), 65.
necromancy 18-19, 21-27, 28, 41-43, 47, 92, 109.

Origen, 38-39, 46, 65, 110, 124, 146.

Palladino, Eusapia, 64.
paradoxa, 101, 116.
paredros (magical helper, see also *ghosts*), 15, 21-22, 33, 37, 39-41, 47.
pareidolia, 67.
Parentalia, 17, 108.
Passover, 86-87.

Paul of Tarsus (see also *empty tomb, eschatology, interpolation*)
  authority, 56-57, 71.
  boasting, 71.
  eschatology, 57-58, 7.
  gospel of, 56-57, 69-71.

Jesus (knowledge of), 70-71, 73-74, 77.
Jesus a "spirit," 108, 110.
letters, 79.
persecutor of early Christians, 74, 83.
resurrection and, 57, 60, 69.
revelations, 70-71, 77.
sanity questioned, 58-59.
seizures, 66.
spirit possession, 72-73.
stigmata, 56.
visions, 54-57, 59, 68, 70-72.

Peter (Cephas), 70, 75, 76-77, 93.
Philinnion, 115, 116-117.
Polycarp to the Philippians, 88.
Porphyry, 113.
possession, 63-64, 72-73, 98.
Prince, Deborah T., 4, 101-102, 106, 122, 125.
Proconsular Acts of Cyprian, 26.
psychosis
  religion and, 59, 63, 64, 67.

relics, 19, 25-26, 92, 143.

resurrection (see also *folklore*)
  accounts similar to ghost lore, 4-8.
  derived from wider culture, 7-9, 152-55.
  doubt among early Christians, 75-76, 82, 88-89, 99-101, 105, 106, 113-14, 127-28.
  central teaching of Christianity, 6-7, 69.
  disputed by early Christians, 7-8, 69, 75-76, 94, 106, 127-28.
  no direct witnesses, 60-61, 94, 102, 105, 106, 121.
  "saints" raised, 100-101.

revenant, 101, 114-117, 125, 134.
Road to Emmaus story, 5, 71, 75, 104-109, 139.

Roman-Jewish War, 9.
Romulus, 118-20.

Sanhedrin, 71, 73-74, 130.
Saul (king of Israel), 23, 24, 43.
schizotypy, 66-67, 73.
seizures
  "kindled," 61-62, 64-65, 66.
  religious conversion following, 66.
  temporary blindness, 66.
Sepher Ha-Razim, 35, 38, 48.
social-scientific perspective, 128.
Society for Psychical Research, 64, 112.

temporal lobe transients, 61-62, 64.
theophagy, 140-41.
tokens left in tomb, 117, 125.
translation (ascension), 91, 120-23, 135.
transliminality, 62-63, 81.

visions (see also *seizures*, *hallucinations*)
  authenticity of, 72-73, 76.
  hallucinations and, 59-60.
  Jesus of, 61.
  "kindled," 61-62, 64-65.
  multiple witnesses, 60.
Virgin Mary
  apparitions of, 61, 124.

Wild Hunt, 20, 126.
women
  as witnesses to empty tomb, 75, 90, 93, 95-98, 99.
  funeral rituals, 131.
  role in early church, 97-98.

www.ingramcontent.com/pod-product-compliance
Lightning Source LLC
LaVergne TN
LVHW051053080426
835508LV00019B/1859